SPIRITUAL AUTHORITY

WHAT'S IT REALLY ALL ABOUT?

RALPH GOOD

outskirts
press

This book is dedicated to all the men and women who humbly lay down their lives to serve the one and only true and living God, proclaiming His redemption from the power of Satan to a lost and dying world!

Table of Contents

Foreword

Bewildered by the abuse and misuse of authority in the local church and staggering from the pain, frustration, and incapacitating hopelessness it caused in my life and others', I spent years studying scripture to find answers, believing, if God's Word is true, the answers can be found in it.I was astonished to find the same Greek word that is used to define the power and authority of God, Jesus Christ, apostles, and believers is also used to define the power and authority of Satan, the devil, the Beast, and the kingdom of darkness!

I simply share from my studies what I have learned about authority, questions I had and explored, and the answers I found that brought healing in my life, freeing me from the condemnation occurring from the abuse and misuse of authority.

Hopefully, this will help you discover God's true purpose for authority, enabling you to fully understand how to exercise the Rights, the Power, and the Authority Jesus Christ restored to man on the cross Satan had stolen from Adam, and, educate you with the ability to discern Satan's perverted use of God's authority for his own glory!

Preface

In this study on authority, we will look at every verse where authority appears, every Greek word authority is translated from, and every word those words are translated to, grouped in common categories.

I compared three translations: King James, New King James, and New Living Translation.

The argument of what translation to use is mute. What is important is understanding the Word of God, so we can be transformed into the full likeness of Christ, in whom we have been made complete, fully realizing how to exercise our rights to the power and authority of the New Covenant believer Jesus Christ established with His own blood on the cross, freely given to all without distinction because of His great love for us!

Reviewing and identifying authority brings clarification, dispels myths, and brings confidence in knowing the truth of God's intended purpose for authority; also, it reveals Satan's misuse of God's authority for his own ambitions, which brought bondage, separation, and death to the human race!

Jesus Christ came that we might have life, release the captives, heal the brokenhearted, and proclaim the favor of the Lord! God's true anointed authorities will always carry out that mission and do even greater things. Jesus Christ has warned us, "See I have told you beforehand, many will come in my Name claiming to be anointed and deceive many, don't let yourselves to be deceived."

CHAPTER 1

AUTHORITY
in the New Testament

King James Bible

Authority (ies) appears 36 times in 33 verses. It's translated from seven Greek words:

New King James Bible

Authority (ies) appears 73 times in 67 verses. It's translated from twelve Greek words:

New Living Translation

Authority (ies) appears 126 times in 113 verses.

The Holy Bible uses the same Greek word (Exousia G1849) to define the power and authority of God, Jesus Christ, apostles, New Covenant believers, Satan, the devil, the Beast, and the kingdom of darkness.

Can you confidently say with full conviction that you have the ability to discern, define, and explain the difference between them, today, at this moment?

Can you truly say you know what Spiritual Authority is?What its boundaries are?What its responsibilities are?If we don't know the true meaning, responsibilities, and boundaries of Spiritual Authority, how can we possibly know if those presenting themselves as authorities in our lives are expressing God's authority or authority scripture attributes to Satan, the devil, the Beast, and the kingdom of darkness, as the same Greek word is used to define all of them? But sometimes, it's translated differently.

Here are a few examples of Exousia G1849, the Greek word most often translated as authority in three translations for easy comparison:

(Explanation: the numbers in the KJV identify the Greek word in *Strong's Concordance* with the English translation underlined in bold print)

Matt. 7:29   English   Greek
                                                                         translation word
KJV   ↓   ↓
²⁹For he taught G2258-G1321 them as one having G2192 **authority G1849**, and not as the scribes G1122.
NKJV
²⁹for He taught them as one having authority, and not as the scribes.
NLT
²⁹for he taught with real authority—quite unlike their teachers of religious law.

Mark 1:27
KJV
²⁷And they were all G3956 amazed G2284, insomuch G5620 that they questioned G4802 among G4314 themselves G848, saying G3004, What G5101 thing is this G3778? What G5101 new G2537 doctrine G1322 is this G5124? for with **authority G1849** commandeth G2004 he even G2532 the unclean G169 spirits G4151, and they do obey G5219 him.
NKJV
²⁷Then they were all amazed, so that they questioned among themselves, saying, "What is this? What new doctrine *is* this? For with authority He commands even the unclean spirits, and they obey Him."

2

NLT [13]Amazement gripped the audience, and they began to discuss what hadhappened. "What sort of new teaching is this?" they asked excitedly. "It has such authority! Even evil spirits obey his orders!"

Matthew 10:1
KJV

[1]And when he had called G4341 unto him his twelve G1427 disciples G3101, he gave G1325 them **power G1849** against unclean G169 spirits G4151, to cast G1544 them out, and to heal G2323 all G3956 manner of sickness G3554 and all G3956 manner of disease G3119.

NKJV

[1]And when He had called His twelve disciples to *Him,* He gave them power *over* unclean spirits, to cast them out, and to heal all kinds of sickness and all kinds of disease.

NLT

[1]Jesus called his twelve disciples together and gave them authority to cast out evil spirits and to heal every kind of disease and illness.

John 1:12
KJV

[12]But as many G3745 as received G2983 him, to them gave G1325 he **power G1849** to become G1096 the sons G5043 of God G2316, even to them that believe G4100 on G1519 his name G3686:

NKJV

[12]But as many as received Him, to them He gave the right to become children of God, to those who believe in His name:

NLT

[12]But to all who believed him and accepted him, he gave the right to become children of God.

Acts 26:18
KJV

[18]To open G455 their eyes G3788, and to turn G1994 them from darkness G4655 to light G5457, and from the **power G1849** of Satan G4567 unto God G2316, that they may receive G2983 forgiveness G859 of sins G266,

SPIRITUAL AUTHORITY: WHAT'S IT REALLY ALL ABOUT?

and inheritance G2819 among G1722 them which are sanctified G37 by faith G4102 that is in me.

NKJV

[18]to open their eyes, *in order* to turn *them* from darkness to light, and *from* the power of Satan to God, that they may receive forgiveness of sins and an inheritance among those who are sanctified by faith in Me.'

NLT

[18]to open their eyes, so they may turn from darkness to light and from the power of Satan to God. Then they will receive forgiveness for their sins and be given a place among God's people, who are set apart by faith in me.'

Colossians 1:13

KJV

[13]Who G3739 hath delivered G4506 us from the **power G1849** of darkness G4655, and hath translated G3179 us into G1519 the kingdom G932 of his dear G26 Son G5207:

NKJV

[13]He has delivered us from the power of darkness and conveyed *us* into the kingdom of the Son of His love,

NLT

[13]For he has rescued us from the kingdom of darkness and transferred us into the Kingdom of his dear Son,

Revelations 13:7

KJV

[7]And it was given G1325 unto him to make G4160 war G4171 with the saints G40, and to overcome G3528 them: and **power G1849** was given G1325 him over G1909 all G3956 kindreds G5443, and tongues G1100, and nations G1484.

NKJV

[7]It was granted to him to make war with the saints and to overcome them. And authority was given him over every tribe, tongue, and nation.

NLT [7]And the beast was allowed to wage war against God's holy people and to conquer them. And he was given authority to rule over every tribe and people and language and nation.

A complete list of Exousia G1849 as translated, which appears 103 times in the NT, is in the Appendix, chapters 2–4.

Let's not assume we know and understand what authority means, or the variety of different roles it has in our lives, each with its own specific functions, responsibilities, and boundaries. More importantly, understand how to appropriately respond when these responsibilities are neglected or legitimate God-given boundaries are violated, causing injury to innocent victims sincerely seeking the will of God.

All of the world's problems began when one of God's delegated authorities overstepped his God-given boundaries and pursued his own ambitions! Lucifer, a created angel, an anointed cherub, put in authority by God, got a vision to become ruler of all creation and have supremacy over the whole universe (Isaiah 14:12–17; Ezekiel 28:11–19). This was not in God's plan for His created propose.In pursuing the fulfillment of his vision, Satan influenced one-third of the angels under his leadership to give up their rightful place and commit to following him. Satan, the authority God created, and the angels who submitted to his leadership when he pursued his own ambitions, were judged by God and banished from heaven for eternity.

Then, Satan, in his craftiness, in pursuit of his vision, influenced the first Adam to give up his rights to the authority God had given to man at creation. This caused man to be separated from God, cursed, and driven out of the Garden of Eden. All humans came under Satan's dominion of darkness when Adam fell to Satan's seduction. Thus, Satan became the ruler of this world instead of man, dooming us to eternal damnation.

But God so loved the world He sent His only Son Jesus. He was the only human not under the power/authority of Satan since the fall of Adam because of the virgin birth. He was anointed to bring Good News to the poor, release the captive, give sight to the blind, let the oppressed go free, proclaim the favor of the Lord, bringing us into full communion with God by His voluntary, sacrificial death on the cross.He defeated the power of Satan on the cross, redeeming us from the kingdom of darkness, adopting us into His kingdom of marvelous light, giving us full rights as sons of the living God, restoring our rights to the authority God had given to man at creation.

He appointed apostles, prophets, evangelists, pastors, and teachers to bring us into full communion with God, teaching us to walk in the fullness of the New Covenant believer Jesus Christ mediated with His death on the cross.Satan, not giving up, and knowing his time is short, sends false apostles, false prophets, and false teachers claiming to be anointed, coming in the name of the Lord, deceiving many to give up their rightful place in God to follow after traditions and teachings of men, enslaving believers in "works of service" to fulfill their own ambitions.

The indescribable pain and suffering inflicted upon humanity by authorities who did not recognize God's plan, exalting themselves, exercising authority over their subjects, making war against their neighbors, slaughtering millions, pursuing their own ambitions of being supreme ruler, cannot be measured by human calculations!Religious cult leaders follow a similar principle, proclaiming themselves to be divinely appointed governing authorities who have a "divine right" to rule, insisting everybody else needs to submit to "their authority" and carry out "works of service" to enlarge their influence over humanity.

At the Sound of the Trumpet

This horrendous abuse and misuse of authority will end as Jesus Christ returns and establishes His kingdom. Satan, the Beast, and False Prophet will be bound in chains and thrown into the bottomless pit. Then, there will be no more war because the fallen delegated authority that deceived the nations will be unable to influence governing authorities to pursue their own selfish ambitions as their father, the devil, did!

Unless we educate ourselves about authority as proclaimed in scripture, we are susceptible to Satan's deceptive use of God's authority. Or, we may unwittingly become a pawn used by him for his purpose of keeping God's people in bondage to the traditions, false teachings, and selfish ambitions of men.

Knowing what role Spiritual Authorities are supposed to have in our lives is the only sure way of discerning the difference between God's intended purpose for authority that brings life, and Satan's twisted use of authority to fulfill his vision of being the supreme ruler that controls mankind for his own purpose, bringing separation and death to God's beloved creation.As we grow in the knowledge of our rights to the power and authority of the New Covenant believer Christ restored to us on the Cross, we will be able to discern the difference between the power and authority of God' kingdom of light and the power and authority of Satan's kingdom of darkness.As we exercise our rights to the power and authority we have been given by Christ, we can walk in freedom from the power and authority of Satan's kingdom of darkness and walk by grace in God's kingdom of marvelous light He has adopted us into and given us full rights as sons of the living God!

CHAPTER 2

Questions about Romans 13:1–2

Romans 13:1–2 KJV

[1]Let every G3956 soul G5590 be subject G5293 unto the higher G5242 powers G1849. For there is no G3756 power G1849 but of God G2316: the powers G1849 that be are ordained G5021 of God G2316.

[2]Whosoever G3588 therefore G5620 resisteth G498 the power G1849, resisteth G436 the ordinance G1296 of God G2316: and they that resist G436 shall receive G2983 to themselves G1438 damnation G2917.

NKJV

[1]Let every soul be subject to the governing authorities. For there is no authority except from God, and the authorities that exist are appointed by God. [2]Therefore whoever resists the authority resists the ordinance of God, and those who resist will bring judgment on themselves.

NLT

[1]Everyone must submit to governing authorities. For all authority comes from God, and those in positions of authority have been placed there by God. [2]So anyone who rebels against authority is rebelling against what God has instituted, and they will be punished.

QUESTION 1

If Romans 13:1–2 is true, why do we teach our children in our Sunday schools to model their lives after the great heroes of the Christian faith who openly defied the authorities God placed in their lives and faced judgment?

Some of these heroes we teach our children to follow are—

Steven, who openly confronted the counsel, including the High Priest for being stiff-necked, resisting the Holy Spirit, killing the prophets, and how they treated God's anointed, the Christ, whom they killed. These people judged him for confronting their misuse of God's authority and dragged him out of town and stoned him to death! We teach our children Stephen is a hero! (Acts, Chapter 7)

Shadrach, Meshach, and Abed-Nego refused to submit to the king's decree and bow to his golden idol, infuriating the king who passed judgment on them for their disobedience and threw them into the fiery furnace. We proclaim them as heroes to our children in our Sunday schools! (Daniel 3)

Daniel openly resisted the decree of the king and faced judgment in the lion's den. We proclaim him as a hero for his defiance of the king's decree and teach our children he is someone to emulate! (Daniel 6)

David, as a lad, with five stones and a slingshot, stood up to a giant as the whole army of God's people trembled in fear, later, ran for his life from God's anointed who was trying to kill him. Not because David did anything wrong or was having a problem with authority. But the authority in his life, Saul, was having a problem with God! And he made a premeditated decision, with 3,000 special forces, to hunt down and kill God's anointed, the forefather of the promised Messiah, killing 85 priests of God, plus their wives and children, for helping David, the man after God's own heart, escape King Saul's malicious judgment! (1 Samuel 17–24)

Peter, who defied the orders of the council and continued to proclaim the name of the Lord, claiming with the other apostles, "It is better to obey God than man!" (Acts 5:29)

Then there's Esther, Moses, Gideon, Paul, John the Baptist, and Jesus Christ Himself, almost always in conflict with the religious authorities God established . . . even calling them a brood of vipers, snakes, and sons of their father, the devil!

All of these and many more, faced judgment for resisting authorities God established, and we proclaim them as heroes to our children as people to model their lives after in our Sunday schools.

To summarize what we teach our children, we teach them to honor the First Commandment. God is to be honored above all, before all, at all times, regardless of the cost, including the cost of their very own lives!

So . . .

At what point in time in the life of believers, from the time we paint murals of these scenes in our nurseries, proclaiming them as the gospel truth, are they required to submit to the implied infallibility of authorities in the local church, and their vision, before their personal relationship with Jesus Christ???

QUESTION 2

Scripture, in Rev. 13, identifies an individual that will rise with great authority and will rule every tribe, tongue, and nation. He will issue laws forbidding anyone to buy and sell unless you take his number, which is 666.

This causes a serious dilemma.

Are we, as Christians, required to submit to the authority scripture says has been given to the Beast?

Are we resisting God and authorities God established if we resist the authority scripture attributes to Satan, the god of this world, the Beast, and the kingdom of darkness? (Detailed in chapter 4 in the Appendix)

Of course NOT!

But refusing to submit will bring judgment of death from the one that scripture says has been given great authority over every tongue, tribe, and nation!

So, did the power and authority scripture says has been given to Satan, the Beast, and the kingdom of darkness originate from God?

Yes, the authority Satan had originated from God, but it was given to Adam at creation. Satan, in his craftiness, stole it to fulfill his own vision; thus, he became the ruler of this world instead of man, bringing mankind under the power and authority of Satan and his kingdom of darkness!

Jesus Christ, the only human being not under the power and authority of Satan because of the virgin birth, refused to violate the First Commandment and withstood Satan's temptations. He made a public spectacle of him on the cross, delivering us from the power and authority of Satan and established the New Covenant, giving us full rights as sons of the living God.

Luke 10:18–20 NKJV

[18]And He said to them, "I saw Satan fall like lightning from heaven. [19]Behold, I give you the authority to trample on serpents and scorpions, and over all the power of the enemy, and nothing shall by any means hurt you. [20]Nevertheless do not rejoice in this, that the spirits are subject to you, but rather rejoice because your names are written in heaven."

Colossians 1:13–14 NKJV

[13]He has delivered us from the power of darkness and conveyed *us* into the kingdom of the Son of His love, [14]in whom we have redemption through His blood, the forgiveness of sins.

Revelations 12:10–11 NKJV

[10]Then I heard a loud voice saying in heaven, "Now salvation, and strength, and the kingdom of our God, and the power of His Christ have come, for the accuser of our brethren, who accused them before our God day and night, has been cast down. [11]And they overcame him by the blood of the Lamb and by the word of their testimony, and they did not love their lives to the death.

James 4:7 NKJV

[7]Therefore submit to God. Resist the devil and he will flee from you.

1 Peter 5:8–9 NKJV

[8]Be sober, be vigilant; because your adversary the devil walks about like a roaring lion, seeking whom he may devour. [9]Resist him, steadfast in the faith, knowing that the same sufferings are experienced by your brotherhood in the world.

QUESTION 3

Jesus Christ used four Greek words to define authority of this world He taught do not belong among His people in Matt. 20:25, Mark 10:42, Luke 22:25 (Detailed study in Chapter 1 in the Appendix). They are as follows from *Strong's* Greek definitions:

G2634
katakurieuo
kat-ak-oo-ree-yoo'-o
From G2596 and G2961; to *lord against,* that is, *control, subjugate:*—exercise dominion over (lordship), be lord over, overcome.

G2715
katexousiazo
kat-ex-oo-see-ad'-zo
From G2596 and G1850; to *have (wield) full privilege over:*—exercise authority.

G2961
kurieuo
koo-ree-you'-o
From G2962; to *rule:*—have dominion over, lord, be lord of, exercise lordship over.

G1850
exousiazo
ex-oo-see-ad'-zo
From G1849; to *control:*—exercise authority upon, bring under the (have) power of.

Would we be resisting God and authorities God established if we resist authorities in the local church, practicing these principles by our obedience to the Lord Jesus Christ who tells us, "It shall not be so among you"?

Do we have a biblical obligation to entrust our lives to authorities practicing these principles?

Is their judgment equal to God's judgment if we don't submit; or, is it from men using fear of judgment as a dominating, controlling mechanism?To submit to, or to allow ourselves to be subdued, overcome, and/or be dominated by authorities practicing these principles brings us again under bondage to principles of this world whose ruler is Satan. If we allow ourselves to become enslaved by the "fear of judgment" they may impose on us, we become useless and separated from God as they become first in our lives instead of God, violating the First Commandment. Thus, we forfeit our ability to walk in the grace given by Jesus Christ, rendering us powerless to exercise our rights to the power, authority, and freedoms He restored to us on the cross. Therefore, we live in defeat!

So, how can authorities in the local church justify passing judgment on God's people for "rebelling against authority" if we follow the teachings of Jesus Christ and refuse to submit to these worldly principles of authority?

QUESTION 4

Protestant/Evangelical/Pentecostal clergy do not believe in or submit to the infallible authority of the pope.

All these clergy believe they have the God-given right and authority, as New Covenant believers, to seek and determine God's will for their own lives through personal prayer and study of scripture, independent from the pope's authority.

So, is the origin of the pope's authority from God? If it is, why don't they submit to him? If the origin of the pope's authority is not from God, an authority exists recognized by millions whose origin has not been established by God!

So then, if the origin of the pope's authority is not from God, and therefore, we don't have to submit to his authority, how many other authorities exist whose origin have not been established by God? And, how can we tell the difference between those who are established by God and those who are not?

Authorities in most Christian denominations, non-denominations, inter-dominations, local churches, and many known religious cults in some way, at least in part, claim Romans 13:1–2 to legitimize their authority as having been established by God and justification to pass judgment on those who refuse to submit to their "application of authority!"

So, what makes the authority of one group more relevant and/or infallible than the authority of another group since they are not in agreement with each other? Some contradict each other. Some taint their followers against authorities in other groups. Some go as far as calling the authority in another group the antichrist. These actions do not reflect the prayer of our Lord in John 17, who established them to bring us into the unity of the faith, the fullness of His redemption, and invited all to sit together at the marriage feast of the Lamb!

When they insist "All authority is of God," which usually means, *my* authority is of God (*not* the pope's), and if you resist me, you will receive judgment. It is a form of dominance akin to the four Greek words Jesus Christ used in defining authority of this world! It certainly does not demonstrate the servanthood Christ Jesus demonstrated with His own life for His servants to follow.

"All authority is of God" includes the authority of the New Covenant believer that gives each and every Christian the right and authority to go to God themselves through the blood of Christ to discern God's will for their own lives! Denying believers this right and authority to discern God's will for their own lives usurps and rejects the authority of Jesus Christ who bought us with His own blood and gave us this right and authority.

So, how can such "Application of Authority" that denies, oppresses, and/or rejects the rights and authority of the New Covenant believer legitimately claim to be of God when He send His Son to die on the cross to establish the rights and authority of the New Covenant believer?

True spiritual authority will always acknowledge, honor, and respect the rights and authority of the New Covenant believer Jesus Christ established when He bought us with His own blood on the cross at Calvary!

QUESTION 5

If all authority is of God as Romans 13:1–2 tells us, why does Jesus Christ repeatedly warn us to take heed, watch out, and be aware of those who either were in or claim to be in God-ordained positions of authority, such as teachers, prophets, and apostles who come in His name?

Matt 7:15–16 NKJV
[15]"Beware of false prophets, who come to you in sheep's clothing, but inwardly they are ravenous wolves. [16]You will know them by their fruits. Do men gather grapes from thornbushes or figs from thistles?

Matt 16:6 NKJV
[6]Then Jesus said to them, "Take heed and beware of the leaven of the Pharisees and the Sadducees."

Matt. 24:4–5 NKJV
[4]And Jesus answered and said to them: "Take heed that no one deceives you. [5]For many will come in My name, saying, 'I am the Christ,' and will deceive many.

Matt 24:23–25 NKJV
[23]"Then if anyone says to you, 'Look, here *is* the Christ!' or 'There!' do not believe *it*. [24]For false christs and false prophets will rise and show great signs and wonders to deceive, if possible, even the elect. [25]See, I have told you beforehand.

Mark 12:38–40 NKJV
[38]Then He said to them in His teaching, "Beware of the scribes, who desire to go around in long robes, *love* greetings in the marketplaces, [39]the best seats in the synagogues, and the best places at feasts, [40]who devour widows' houses, and for a pretense make long prayers. These will receive greater condemnation."

Mark 13:21–23 NKJV
[21]"Then if anyone says to you, 'Look, here *is* the Christ!' or, 'Look, *He is* there!' do not believe it. [22]For false christs and false prophets will rise and show signs and wonders to deceive, if possible, even the elect. [23]But take heed; see, I have told you all things beforehand.

Luke 17:22–23 NKJV

22Then He said to the disciples, "The days will come when you will desire to see one of the days of the Son of Man, and you will not see *it.* 23And they will say to you, 'Look here!' or 'Look there!' Do not go after *them* or follow *them.*

Luke 21:8–9 NKJV

8And He said: "Take heed that you not be deceived. For many will come in My name, saying, 'I am *He,*' and, 'The time has drawn near.' Therefore do not go after them. 9But when you hear of wars and commotions, do not be terrified; for these things must come to pass first, but the end *will not come* immediately."

1 Corinthians 7:23 NKJV

23You were bought at a price; do not become slaves of men.

2 Corinthians 11:3–4 NKJV

3But I fear, lest somehow, as the serpent deceived Eve by his craftiness, so your minds may be corrupted from the simplicity that is in Christ. 4For if he who comes preaches another Jesus whom we have not preached, or *if* you receive a different spirit which you have not received, or a different gospel which you have not accepted—you may well put up with it!

2 Corinthians 11:13–15 NKJV

13For such *are* false apostles, deceitful workers, transforming themselves into apostles of Christ. 14And no wonder! For Satan himself transforms himself into an angel of light. 15Therefore *it is* no great thing if his ministers also transform themselves into ministers of righteousness, whose end will be according to their works.

Galatians 2:4–5 NKJV

4And *this occurred* because of false brethren secretly brought in (who came in by stealth to spy out our liberty which we have in Christ Jesus, that they might bring us into bondage), 5to whom we did not yield submission even for an hour, that the truth of the gospel might continue with you.

Galatians 5:1 NKJV
[1]Stand fast therefore in the liberty by which Christ has made us free, and do not be entangled again with a yoke of bondage.

Ephesians 4:14 NKJV
[14]. . . that we should no longer be children, tossed to and fro and carried about with every wind of doctrine, by the trickery of men, in the cunning craftiness of deceitful plotting,

Ephesians 5:6–7 NKJV
[6]Let no one deceive you with empty words, for because of these things the wrath of God comes upon the sons of disobedience. [7]Therefore do not be partakers with them.

Colossians 2:8–10 NKJV
[8]Beware lest anyone cheat you through philosophy and empty deceit, according to the tradition of men, according to the basic principles of the world, and not according to Christ. [9]For in Him dwells all the fullness of the Godhead bodily; [10]and you are complete in Him, who is the head of all principality and power.

Colossians 2:18–19 NKJV
[18]Let no one cheat you of your reward, taking delight in *false* humility and worship of angels, intruding into those things which he has not seen, vainly puffed up by his fleshly mind, [19]and not holding fast to the Head, from whom all the body, nourished and knit together by joints and ligaments, grows with the increase *that is* from God.

1 Timothy 4:1–3 NKJV
[1]Now the Spirit expressly says that in latter times some will depart from the faith, giving heed to deceiving spirits and doctrines of demons, [2]speaking lies in hypocrisy, having their own conscience seared with a hot iron, [3]forbidding to marry, *and commanding* to abstain from foods which God created to be received with thanksgiving by those who believe and know the truth.

2 Peter 2:1–3 NKJV

¹But there were also false prophets among the people, even as there will be false teachers among you, who will secretly bring in destructive heresies, even denying the Lord who bought them, *and* bring on themselves swift destruction. ²And many will follow their destructive ways, because of whom the way of truth will be blasphemed. ³By covetousness they will exploit you with deceptive words; for a long time their judgment has not been idle, and their destruction does not slumber.

1 John 4:1 NKJV

¹Beloved, do not believe every spirit, but test the spirits, whether they are of God; because many false prophets have gone out into the world.

These scriptures can cause serious suspicions, and rightly so!

If we listen to false apostles, false prophets, false teachers who come in His name (and they will not tell you if they are false; they may not even be aware of that), we will be led away from God to follow man, violating the First Commandment. This opens the door for Satan to bring condemnation and destruction into our lives!

So who are the real authorities in the body of Christ? (We address that in the next chapter.)

CHAPTER 3

Who Are the Governing Authorities?

Many falsely believe and proclaim the governing authorities in the local church are those in the fivefold ministry, such as apostles, prophets, evangelists, pastors, and teachers.

This false belief opens the door for false teachers, false apostles, and false prophets Jesus Christ warned us about who try to exercise authority over believers and draw them after themselves!

The Bible says in Ephesians 4:11, NKJV, "He Himself gave some to be apostles, some prophets, some evangelists, and some pastors and teachers."

He Himself, being the Lord Jesus Christ, He is the governing authority who appointed them; giving them their purpose and guidelines how to fulfill that purpose in His divinely inspired written Word. Yes, some of their responsibility is to govern, but within boundaries of the servanthood Jesus Christ our Lord demonstrated to bring hope to the poor, freedom to the captive, sight to the blind, release of the oppressed . . . turning people from the power of Satan to God. Utilizing principles scripture identifies as authority of this world, whose ruler is Satan, to build the body of Christ, that's not of this world, has been outlawed by the one who appointed them!

Scripture Identifies Jesus Christ As the Governing Authority!

John 1:1–4 NKJV

¹In the beginning was the Word, and the Word was with God, and the Word was God. ²He was in the beginning with God. ³All things were made through Him, and without Him nothing was made that was made. ⁴In Him was life, and the life was the light of men.

Matt 28:18–20 NKJV

¹⁸And Jesus came and spoke to them, saying, "All authority has been given to Me in heaven and on earth. ¹⁹Go therefore and make disciples of all the nations, baptizing them in the name of the Father and of the Son and of the Holy Spirit, ²⁰teaching them to observe all things that I have commanded you; and lo, I am with you always, *even* to the end of the age." Amen.

Ephesians 1:15–23 NKJV

¹⁵Therefore I also, after I heard of your faith in the Lord Jesus and your love for all the saints, ¹⁶do not cease to give thanks for you, making mention of you in my prayers: ¹⁷that the God of our Lord Jesus Christ, the Father of glory, may give to you the spirit of wisdom and revelation in the knowledge of Him, ¹⁸the eyes of your understanding being enlightened; that you may know what is the hope of His calling, what are the riches of the glory of His inheritance in the saints, ¹⁹and what *is* the exceeding greatness of His power toward us who believe, according to the working of His mighty power ²⁰which He worked in Christ when He raised Him from the dead and seated *Him* at His right hand in the heavenly *places,* ²¹far above all principality and power and might and dominion, and every name that is named, not only in this age but also in that which is to come.
²²And He put all *things* under His feet, and gave Him *to be* head over all *things* to the church, ²³which is His body, the fullness of Him who fills all in all.

Ephesians 4:1–6 NKJV

¹I, therefore, the prisoner of the Lord, beseech you to walk worthy of the

calling with which you were called, [2]with all lowliness and gentleness, with longsuffering, bearing with one another in love, [3]endeavoring to keep the unity of the Spirit in the bond of peace. [4]*There is* one body and one Spirit, just as you were called in one hope of your calling; [5]one Lord, one faith, one baptism; [6]one God and Father of all, who *is* above all, and through all, and in you all.

Colossians 1:15–18 NKJV

[15]He is the image of the invisible God, the firstborn over all creation. [16]For by Him all things were created that are in heaven and that are on earth, visible and invisible, whether thrones or dominions or principalities or powers. All things were created through Him and for Him. [17]And He is before all things, and in Him all things consist. [18]And He is the head of the body, the church, who is the beginning, the firstborn from the dead, that in all things He may have the preeminence.

Philippians 2:9–11 NKJV

[9]Therefore God also has highly exalted Him and given Him the name which is above every name, [10]that at the name of Jesus every knee should bow, of those in heaven, and of those on earth, and of those under the earth, [11]and *that* every tongue should confess that Jesus Christ *is* Lord, to the glory of God the Father.

So, when Paul wrote in Romans 13:1–2, "Let every soul be subject to the governing authorities," he was telling us, "Let everybody be subject to Christ!" For He has preeminence above all, created all, is in all and through all, and He appointed all governing authorities to be subject to Himself for He is the King of kings and Lord of lords now and forever will be.

Nowhere is it written in scripture, to my knowledge, where a believer is to violate the First Commandment and put any delegated authority above and before their personal relationship with Jesus Christ! False teachers will draw men after themselves.

Luke 12:4–5 NKJV

[4]"Dear friends, don't be afraid of those who want to kill your body; they cannot do any more to you after that. [5]But I'll tell you whom to fear. Fear God, who has the power to kill you and then throw you into hell. Yes, He's the one to fear.

Matthew 4:10 NKJV

[10]Then Jesus said to him, "Away with you, Satan! For it is written, *'You shall worship the Lord your God, and Him only you shall serve.'"*

Matthew 7:21 NKJV

[21]"Not everyone who says to Me, 'Lord, Lord,' shall enter the kingdom of heaven, but he who does the will of My Father in heaven."

Matthew 10:38 NKJV

[38]And he who does not take his cross and follow after Me is not worthy of Me.

Matthew 16:24 NKJV

[24]Then Jesus said to His disciples, "If anyone desires to come after Me, let him deny himself, and take up his cross, and follow Me."

Matthew 22:37–40 NKJV

[37]Jesus said to him, "'You shall love the Lord your God with all your heart, with all your soul, and with all your mind.' [38]This is *the* first and great commandment. [39]And *the* second *is* like it: 'You shall love your neighbor as yourself.' [40]On these two commandments hang all the Law and the Prophets."

1 Peter 2:21 NKJV

[21]For to this you were called, because Christ also suffered for us, leaving us an example, that you should follow His steps.

Galatians 4:17 NLT

[17]Those false teachers are so eager to win your favor, but their intentions are not good. They are trying to shut you off from me so that you will pay attention only to them.

First and foremost, the true spiritual authorities in the body of Christ are our brothers. Brothers, because we are all sons of the Most High! Because we are all sons, adopted into the body of Christ; we are nothing more than brothers with a variety of different gifts to edify the brethren. None of these gifts make one more special than another, or gives them the authority to dominate over another; rather, it gives each a different ability to serve one another in love to the glory of God!

As brothers, we are instructed to love one another, honor one another, respect one another, treat one another with dignity, look out for one another, and serve one another.

Matthew 23:8–12 NKJV

[8]But you, do not be called 'Rabbi'; for One is your Teacher, the Christ, and you are all brethren. [9]Do not call anyone on earth your father; for One is your Father, He who is in heaven. [10]And do not be called teachers; for One is your Teacher, the Christ. [11]But he who is greatest among you shall be your servant. [12]And whoever exalts himself will be humbled, and he who humbles himself will be exalted.

Romans 13:8–10 NKJV

[8]Owe no one anything except to love one another, for he who loves another has fulfilled the law. [9]For the commandments, *"You shall not commit adultery," "You shall not murder," "You shall not steal," "You shall not bear false witness," "You shall not covet,"* and if *there is* any other commandment, are *all* summed up in this saying, namely, *"You shall love your neighbor as yourself."* [10]Love does no harm to a neighbor; therefore love *is* the fulfillment of the law.

1 Corinthians 13:1–8 NKJV

[1]Though I speak with the tongues of men and of angels, but have not love, I have become sounding brass or a clanging cymbal. [2]And though I have *the gift of* prophecy, and understand all mysteries and all knowledge, and though I have all faith, so that I could remove mountains, but have not love, I am nothing. [3]And though I bestow all my goods to feed *the poor,* and though I give my body to be burned, but have not love, it profits me nothing. [4]Love suffers long *and* is kind; love does not envy; love does not parade itself, is not puffed up; [5]does not behave rudely, does not seek its own, is not provoked, thinks no evil; [6]does not rejoice in iniquity, but rejoices in the truth; [7]bears all things, believes all things, hopes all things, endures all things.
[8]Love never fails.

Ephesians 3:14–19 NKJV

[14]For this reason I bow my knees to the Father of our Lord Jesus Christ, [15]from whom the whole family in heaven and earth is named, [16]that He would grant you, according to the riches of His glory, to be strengthened with might through His Spirit in the inner man, [17]that Christ may dwell in your hearts through faith; that you, being rooted and grounded in love, [18]may be able to comprehend with all the saints what *is* the width and length and depth and height—[19]to know the love of Christ which passes knowledge; that you may be filled with all the fullness of God.

1 Peter 1:22 NKJV

[22]Since you have purified your souls in obeying the truth through the Spirit in sincere love of the brethren, love one another fervently with a pure heart.

2 Peter 1:5–9 NKJV

[5]But also for this very reason, giving all diligence, add to your faith virtue, to virtue knowledge, [6]to knowledge self-control, to self-control perseverance, to perseverance godliness, [7]to godliness brotherly kindness, and to brotherly kindness love. [8]For if these things are yours and abound, *you will*

be neither barren nor unfruitful in the knowledge of our Lord Jesus Christ. ⁹For he who lacks these things is shortsighted, even to blindness, and has forgotten that he was cleansed from his old sins.

1 John 2:3–6 NKJV

³Now by this we know that we know Him, if we keep His commandments. ⁴He who says, "I know Him," and does not keep His commandments, is a liar, and the truth is not in him. ⁵But whoever keeps His word, truly the love of God is perfected in him. By this we know that we are in Him. ⁶He who says he abides in Him ought himself also to walk just as He walked.

1 John 2:9–11 NKJV

⁹He who says he is in the light, and hates his brother, is in darkness until now. ¹⁰He who loves his brother abides in the light, and there is no cause for stumbling in him. ¹¹But he who hates his brother is in darkness and walks in darkness, and does not know where he is going, because the darkness has blinded his eyes.

1 John 4:15–16 NKJV

¹⁵Whoever confesses that Jesus is the Son of God, God abides in him, and he in God. ¹⁶And we have known and believed the love that God has for us. God is love, and he who abides in love abides in God, and God in him.

James 3:13–18 NKJV

¹³Who *is* wise and understanding among you? Let him show by good conduct *that* his works *are done* in the meekness of wisdom. ¹⁴But if you have bitter envy and self-seeking in your hearts, do not boast and lie against the truth. ¹⁵This wisdom does not descend from above, but *is* earthly, sensual, demonic. ¹⁶For where envy and self-seeking *exist,* confusion and every evil thing *are* there. ¹⁷But the wisdom that is from above is first pure, then peaceable, gentle, willing to yield, full of mercy and good fruits, without partiality and without hypocrisy. ¹⁸Now the fruit of righteousness is sown in peace by those who make peace.

From brothers, who do these things, God appoints the ones He calls to lead His people as an example to follow. When the Lord Jesus Christ appoints overseers in the church, He does not take away their free will. Every day, they must choose to walk in His footsteps.

Unfortunately, some do not continue to make that choice to follow God!

Galatians 1:6–9 NKJV

[6]I marvel that you are turning away so soon from Him who called you in the grace of Christ, to a different gospel, [7]which is not another; but there are some who trouble you and want to pervert the gospel of Christ. [8]But even if we, or an angel from heaven, preach any other gospel to you than what we have preached to you, let him be accursed. [9]As we have said before, so now I say again, if anyone preaches any other gospel to you than what you have received, let him be accursed.

Galatians 4:8–9 NKJV

[8]But then, indeed, when you did not know God, you served those which by nature are not gods. [9]But now after you have known God, or rather are known by God, how *is it that* you turn again to the weak and beggarly elements, to which you desire again to be in bondage?

1 Timothy 1:5–7 NKJV

[5]Now the purpose of the commandment is love from a pure heart, *from* a good conscience, and *from* sincere faith, [6]from which some, having strayed, have turned aside to idle talk, [7]desiring to be teachers of the law, understanding neither what they say nor the things which they affirm.

1 Timothy 4:1–2 NLT

[1]Now the Holy Spirit tells us clearly that in the last times some will turn away from the true faith; they will follow deceptive spirits and teachings that come from demons. [2]These people are hypocrites and liars, and their consciences are dead.

Rev. 2:4–5 NKJV

[4]Nevertheless I have *this* against you, that you have left your first love. [5]Remember therefore from where you have fallen; repent and do the first works, or else I will come to you quickly and remove your lampstand from its place—unless you repent.

In the Gospels, Jesus Christ spoke against many in positions of authority who considered themselves righteous, condemning their actions.In the Old Testament, almost all prophets spoke against authorities that did not follow God's instructions. I will include one of them here.

Ezekiel 34:1–6 NKJV

[1]And the word of the Lord came to me, saying, [2]"Son of man, prophesy against the shepherds of Israel, prophesy and say to them, 'Thus says the Lord GOD to the shepherds: "Woe to the shepherds of Israel who feed themselves! Should not the shepherds feed the flocks? [3]You eat the fat and clothe yourselves with the wool; you slaughter the fatlings, *but* you do not feed the flock. [4]The weak you have not strengthened, nor have you healed those who were sick, nor bound up the broken, nor brought back what was driven away, nor sought what was lost; but with force and cruelty you have ruled them. [5]So they were scattered because *there was* no shepherd; and they became food for all the beasts of the field when they were scattered. [6]My sheep wandered through all the mountains, and on every high hill; yes, My flock was scattered over the whole face of the earth, and no one was seeking or searching *for them.*"

So, the question comes to my mind, if God, in His Word, is condemning authorities He appointed for not doing the work He has appointed them to do, what expectations are we to have of authorities we are to serve?

Obviously, we do not want to be touching God's anointed or do them harm. That's wrong. However, we do not want to give a pass to false teachers, false apostles, and false prophets who come in His name and allow ourselves to be deceived by them, just because they come in His name, claiming to be anointed! To allow ourselves to be

deceived is to revolt against the teaching of Jesus Christ who tells us, "Don't let yourself be deceived!"

Jesus Christ commended the Ephesians for having tested the works of those who claimed to be apostles and found them liars (Rev. 2:2). Therefore, it is OK the test the works of those claiming to be apostles.

Yes! It is hard to test the works of apostles, prophets, and teachers if we don't know what their works are supposed to be. This lack of knowledge makes it difficult to discern between the true apostles, prophets, and teachers we are not to touch, and the false ones Jesus Christ repeatedly warned us not to follow!

But, wait a minute!

All true apostles, prophets, and teachers in the body of Christ are brothers first and are not exempt from keeping the royal law of loving one another! Therefore, we can test if they still love, honor, and respect us as brothers if we don't yield (as yes-men) to doing "works of service" to fulfill their own ambitions, or, if we are condemned for "having a problem with authority" when we exercise our God-given authority as New Covenant believers and say NO (Matt. 5:27) to their craftiness, when exercising authority over us, to get us to fulfill their vision!

We are to "test all things to see if they are of God (1 John 4:1; 1 Thess. 5:21)." Therefore, we can test if apostles, prophets, and teachers are bringing us closer to our creator, growing us into the fullness of Christ, enabling us to exercise the rights and authority we have been given as New Covenant believers, or, getting us to give up our rights as adopted children of the Most High and do "works of service" to build their organization as if we are, "giving to God." But in reality, we got deceived into following man's vision instead of God's. The latter has similarities to Satan deceiving one-third of the angels God Himself put under his leadership. He caused them to sin against God by getting them to give up their rightful place to submit to his vision, bringing them under judgment of hell for eternity (2 Peter 2:4; Jude 1:6).

Frankly, if it's expected we acknowledge them as authorities, established by God, submit to them, give them our tithe (so we will not be cursed by God), why would it be wrong to expect them to have good fruit consistent with the works of the one they claim appointed them?

For example, if we have a house with a leaky roof, we hire someone to fix it for us. If they tell us they know how to do roofing, it's OK to expect them to be able to do the job we hire them for! If they don't do the job right, we don't pay and/or consider them bogus businessmen or fly-by-night roofers.

If we are sick and go to a doctor, we expect the doctor to know what treatment is needed. If they don't know for sure, we expect them to do tests and send us to a specialist. It is never wrong to question the authority of the doctor and get a second opinion. In many cases, it is the right thing to do as they are human and make mistakes.

Obviously, our soul is more important than our bodies; it lasts forever . . . in heaven or hell! Our bodies return to dust even with the best medical treatment available from multiple teams of doctors.

So, why would we "have a problem with authority," if we question authorities in the local church, who are human and make mistakes and seek a second opinion on spiritual matters from trusted, qualified individuals BEFORE we submit to their "application of authority"? Especially since our Lord repeatedly warned us, "Take heed, watch out and be aware; don't let yourselves be deceived by those who come in my name!"

We, as believers, who do works of service, give our tithes and offerings to support the Lord's work, have every right to expect authorities whose ministries benefit from our giving to the Lord to be doing the Lord's work and maintain the characteristics set forth in scripture for leadership and hold to accountability all leaders in the local church to that standard of leadership. Not standards *we* come up with, but characteristics set forth by God in His written Word, who appointed them, whose authority they claim to represent!

A chart from *A Theology of Church Leadership* (Zondervan) lists 28 such characteristics, and gives a brief explanation of each.

Qualifications for Leadership

Scripture
Qualification
Explanation

Titus 1:5–9

1. Above reproach
    Not open to censure; having unimpeachable integrity
2. Husband of one wife
    A one-wife kind of man, not a philanderer (doesn't necessarily rule out widowers or divorced men).
3. Having believing children
    Children are Christians, not incorrigible or unruly.
4. Not self-willed
    Not arrogantly self-satisfied
5. Not quick-tempered
    Not prone to anger or irascible
6. Not addicted to wine
    Not fond of wine or drunk
7. Not pugnacious
    Not contentious or quarrelsome
8. Not a money-lover
    Not greedy for money
9. Hospitable
    A stranger-lover, generous to guests
10. Lover of good
    Loving goodness
11. Sensible
    Self-controlled, sane, temperate
12. Just
    Righteous, upright, aligned with right
13. Devout
    Responsible in fulfilling moral obligations to God and man
14. Self-controlled
    Restrained, under control

15. Holding fast the Word

    Committed to God's Word as authoritative

16. Able to teach sound doctrine

    Calling others to wholeness through teaching God's Word

17. Able to refute objections

    Convincing those who speak against the truth

Additional from 1 Timothy 3:1–7

18. Temperate

    Calm and collected in spirit; sober

19. Gentle

    Fair, equitable, not insisting on his own rights

20. Able to manage household

    A good leader in his own family

21. Not a new convert

    Not a new Christian

22. Well thought of

    Good representative of Christ

Additional from 1 Peter 5:1–4

23. Willingly, not under compulsion

    Not serving against his will

24. According to God (in some Greek texts)

    By God's appointment

25. Not for shameful gain

    Not money-motivated

26. Not lording it over the flock

    Not dominating in his area of ministry (a shepherd is to lead, not drive the flock)

27. As an example

    A pleasure to follow because of his Christian example

28. As accountable to the Chief Shepherd

    Motivated by the crown to be gained—authority to reign with Christ

If people are promoted to positions of authority in the local church because they submit to the vision of authorities, without having knowledgeable understanding of these fundamental requirements and accountability to live by them, the scriptural foundation for spiritual authority in the local church has been disregarded. This nullifies their claims of being founded on scripture, thereby, invalidating their legitimacy as true spiritual authorities in the local church.

As a result of this departure from the scriptural foundation for spiritual authority, unnecessary injury will greatly increase to innocent victims who have no recourse to address offences as no one will hear anything negative said about leadership! For, "all authority is of God and whoever resists them is resisting what God has established and brings judgment on themselves Romans (13:1-2 NKJV)!" This misuse of Romans 13:1–2 rejects the biblical model of reconciliation, negates accountability of leadership, projects culpability, and oppresses with unjustifiable obligation on the victim for the injury received from conduct inconsistent with someone representing the hands and feet of Jesus Christ!

When confronted, many have said, "I'm the authority; I can do what I want!" This is absolutely true! God does not take away the free will of anybody!

Hopefully, they want to release the oppressed, set the captive free, bind up the broken, heal the sick, etc.; thus, fulfilling the royal law of loving one another as Jesus Christ first loved us, who gave Himself for us while we were yet sinners, setting the example for His servants to follow, who appointed them to do His work, proclaiming the fullness of His redemption from the power of Satan!

But if they exercise their free will to reject the boundaries of spiritual authority, as Lucifer did, and use force and cruelty to rule the people, placing heavy burdens on them, introducing false doctrines to exploit, enslave, and exercise authority over them, separating people from God to fulfill their vision, we, who know the Word, must stand for truth and liberate the little lambs from the impudence of such beasts! For we know! The Good Shepherd does not do that!

No! We are not resisting God when we resist authorities like that as they want us to think when they quote from Romans 13:1–2, "all authority is of God," to legitimize exercising authority over us and "whoever resists them brings judgment on themselves" to justify their condemnation for being resisted! Rather, Ephesians 6:12 applies!

We wrestle against such rulers, authorities, and powers who, like Lucifer, reject the boundaries of spiritual authority Jesus Christ established, and demand loyalty to themselves and their vision as Nebuchadnezzar did and had those who refused to submit thrown into a fiery furnace.

No! No! No!

We are *not* resisting God and the authorities God established by our obedience to the First Commandment by maintaining our loyalty to the one and only true God who sent His Son to die on the cross, reconciling the world to Himself by His blood removing the separation between God and man caused by the fallen delegated authority (Lucifer) pursing his own ambitions!

When Jesus Christ gave the Great Commission (Matt. 28:19–20 NKJV), "Go therefore and make disciples of all the nations, baptizing them in the name of the Father and of the Son and of the Holy Spirit, teaching them to observe all things that I have commanded you," this mandate includes teaching everyone to honor, respect, and obverse the First and Great Commandment!

Therefore, true spiritual authorities will *never* lead anyone to violate the First Commandment, separating them from God, leading to their ultimate destruction. That's what the serpent did to Adam and Eve in the Garden of Eden!

Now then, we are ambassadors for Christ, as though God were pleading through us: we implore you on Christ's behalf, be reconciled to God (2 Corinthians 5:20 NKJV).

If the body of Christ is unwilling to address such abuse and misuse of authority in the local church, we are disingenuous before God when we quote the famous revival prayer.

2 Chronicles 7:14 NKJV

[14]"if My people who are called by My name will humble themselves, and pray and seek My face, and turn from their wicked ways, then I will hear from heaven, and will forgive their sin and heal their land."

CHAPTER 4

AUTHORITY
for the Common Good

In a fallen world ruled by Satan, who deceives the nations, causing them to wage war against each other, sometimes I have to wonder if authorities really understand they are God's ministers appointed for the common good of all people.

Satan, the god of this world, is always influencing, or at least attempting to influence, societies with the help of some in government, to turn them away from God leading to their disintegration. It is a constant battle for the righteous to maintain godliness in society as unseen evil forces are continually undermining the spiritual unity and well-being of the brethren.

Moses struggled with this issue. As he was getting ready to lead the children of Israel into the Promised Land, ten of the twelve leaders chosen to spy out the land stirred the people against possessing the rights and blessings of the Promised Land, causing them to wander in the wilderness for forty years. (Numbers ch.13–14)

The Old Testament prophets continually confronted leaders of Israel, calling them back to God, pleading with them to honor His commandants, reminding them to do what is just and righteous in the eyes of God.

Nothing can be more reprehensible and painful then the humiliation and betrayal of trust caused by abuse and misuse of authority. David understood this well. In the Psalms, he cried out to the Lord many times for

God's help who sustained him when he was running from God's anointed who was trying to kill him. Not because David was at fault, but King Saul had a problem with God. Twice, David had the opportunity to take Saul's life, but he did not raise his hand against God's anointed, even though he was unjustly condemned and chased like a wild animal.

Saul and David were never reconciled. Not because of David, but Saul was unrepentant. Therefore, David had to protect himself and ran for his life from the authority that had no problem trying to kill the man after God's own heart.

Other authorities had similar problems.

King Herod, when told by the Wise Men a king had been born, knew it was the Messiah, for he asked the religious leaders where the Messiah would be born. They told him Bethlehem. He sent his soldiers to kill all the boys younger than two in his attempt to kill the Messiah! (Matt. 2 NLT)

The corrupt sons of Eli the High Priest demanded the people give more than God required. If the people did not give it, they took it by force (1 Samuel 2:12–14 NKJV).

1 Chronicles 21:1–2 NKJV
[1]Now Satan stood up against Israel, and moved David to number Israel. [2]So David said to Joab and to the leaders of the people, "Go, number Israel from Beersheba to Dan, and bring the number of them to me that I may know *it*."

Rehoboam, King David's grandson, tried to enslave Israel so he could live extravagantly at their expense. They refused to submit and told him:

1 Kings 12:16 NKJV
"What share have we in David? We have no inheritance in the son of Jesse. To your tents, O Israel! Now, see to your own house, O David!"

Rehoboam, angered by their rejection, raised an army of one hundred eighty thousand men to force them into submission.

God send Shemaiah, the prophet, to intervene and told them not to fight against their brethren and send the army home (1 Kings 12:24).

Israel became a divided nation.

Then we have Saul. A bright young student of the Word, in total agreement with and obedience to the authorities in his life, he persecuted the early Church with unrelenting zeal. On the road to Damascus, carrying out his commission he received from the elders, Jesus Christ confronted him saying, "Saul, Saul, why do you persecute me?"

Jesus Christ intervened on behalf of the His Church, challenging someone who was misusing authority to destroy it instead of edifying the people of the Church! Saul, who later became Paul, acknowledged he was acting ignorantly in unbelief (1 Tim. 1:13).

Jesus Christ acknowledged there will be abuse and misuse of authority in Luke 12:1–12; Matthew 21:33–42; Matthew 24:45–51; 2 Peter 2:1–3.

John 16:1–4 NKJV

[1]"These things I have spoken to you, that you should not be made to stumble. [2]They will put you out of the synagogues; yes, the time is coming that whoever kills you will think that he offers God service. [3]And these things they will do to you because they have not known the Father nor Me. [4]But these things I have told you, that when the time comes, you may remember that I told you of them.

Confronting and standing against abuse and misuse of authority is never easy, even dangerous! John the Baptist was beheaded. Stephen was stoned to death. Many Old Testament prophets were killed. All martyrs of the Christian faith refused to bow to those who did not recognize the sovereignty of Almighty God and His plan of redemption from the power of Satan.

Confronting abuse and misuse of authority is not touching God's anointed, as some would have you to believe. If it is, most Old Testament prophets were touching God's anointed. There is no indication they were. As a matter of fact, the content of those verses was directed toward those in authority.

Psalms 105:13-15

When they went from one nation to another, And from *one* kingdom to another people, ¹⁴He permitted no man to do them wrong; Yes, He rebuked kings for their sakes, ¹⁵*Saying,* "Do not touch My anointed ones, And do My prophets no harm."

Whether the abuse and misuse of authority was intentional as some leaders of Israel committed, or in ignorance and unbelief like the violence Saul committed against the church, or simply good-hearted people with the sincerest intentions who don't understand the boundaries and responsibilities of spiritual authority Jesus Christ established, they succumb to Satan's tactics; to the victims, the pain hurts just the same. The pain is not a reflection of the victim, who is just learning the Bible and submits to authority as required (Romans 13:1–2) to avoid judgment. It reflects the fruit of authorities that didn't understand and/or failed to acknowledge and submit to the governing authority of Christ Jesus who appointed them to do His work!

Of course, all the spiritual people insist the victims need to be held accountable to forgive. And, yes, they do need to work through the process of forgiveness and healing and come to the realization the actions chosen by authorities have nothing to do with who they are! But that does not fix the problem or restore unity and fellowship among the brethren, nor does it provide justice for the victim as required by God in scripture.

The authorities need to be held accountable to maintain an example of humility and godliness in their treatment of others in their care as well (1 Tim. 5:19–20; James 3:1–2; Peter 2:1). Otherwise, they will do the same to the next person, and the next person, and the next person, and may not be aware of their blindness. All these injured people will need to walk through the process of forgiveness and healing. But nobody wants to address the source of the problem to stop it as they refuse to hear anything negative said against those in authority. This negligent refusal to hold leadership accountable to maintain a biblical standard gives Satan an open door into the lives of unsuspecting people who, with sincerity, unknowingly come to church and submit to such authorities.

Instead of bringing healing, deliverance, and wholeness to a person, they place stumbling blocks and heavy burdens on the people, making it more difficult for them to obtain the grace to walk in the fullness of the New Covenant Jesus Christ died on the cross to give them.

If these injuries are not appropriately navigated (some don't have the skills to do that), a root of bitterness will grow and defile many (Heb. 12:14–15), causing separation from God, leading to their ultimate destruction. This is the work of the powers of hell, whose ruler is Satan, who came to steal, kill, and destroy!

Ephesians 4:11–13 NKJV
[11]And He Himself gave some *to be* apostles, some prophets, some evangelists, and some pastors and teachers, [12]for the equipping of the saints for the work of ministry, for the edifying of the body of Christ, [13]till we all come to the unity of the faith and of the knowledge of the Son of God, to a perfect man, to the measure of the stature of the fullness of Christ;

The fullness of Christ is love; Therefore, it all starts here!

Matthew 22:37-40 NKJV
[37]Jesus said to him, " *'You shall love the Lord your God with all your heart, with all your soul, and with all your mind.'* [38]This is *the* first and great commandment. [39]And *the* second *is* like it: *'You shall love your neighbor as yourself.'* [40]On these two commandments hang all the Law and the Prophets."

Now, there seems to be some confusion among Christians about the requirements of the Law. Many believe since we are not under the Law, we don't have to love one another. This belief strongly manifests itself in the way we treat one another. My goodness! Well, I will *not* go there!

Jesus did fulfill the requirements of the Law, sacrificing His own blood for our sins once and for all; therefore, we do not need to offer blood sacrifices to obtain forgiveness for our sins anymore as the Law required. However, He said, "A new commandment I give to you, that you love one another; as I have loved you, that you also love one another. By this all will know

39

that you are My disciples, if you have love for one another" (Matthew 13:34–35 NKJV).

So now, instead of just loving those who love us, we need to love those who do *not* love us! Treat them kindly, justly, with respect and dignity, as Christ loved us while we were yet sinners.

Stephen expressed this kind of love as the religious people were stoning him to death, realizing their minds were blinded by Satan, saying, "Father, do not charge them with this sin!"

Can we say we love like that?

Can we forgive those who lie about us? Misunderstand us? Despitefully use us?

Can we fall on our face and pray, "Father, do not charge them with this sin," and continue to treat them with dignity and respect as a human being?

Most of us expect that from others if we sin against them; and, may even take offence if we don't get it right away.

So, why do we want to nail them to a piece of wood till every drop of blood falls to the ground like the unloving religious people who had Jesus Christ nailed to a piece of wood we call, "The Cross"?

Our sin already nailed Jesus Christ to the cross—We don't need to do that to anybody else.

Can we be identified as His disciples by our expression of love toward those who try to destroy us? I am not saying we have to let them do that. David did not hang around and allow God's anointed destroy him! He ran for his life.

Do we, who are spiritual, try to restore a brother in the spirit of gentleness if someone is caught in a trespass; or, do we want to pass judgment and stone him to death as the religious people did to Stephen, who really believed in their hearts were doing to the will of God?

Well, maybe we do not really want to stone him—just drive him out of the church by treating him so badly he leaves.

That's what King Saul did to David, the man after God's own heart! Then, chased him for the rest of his life trying to destroy him.

It appears King Saul's personality of "I'm in charge, I'm the king, I'm the authority, I can do what I want (which got him rejected as king), was

Satan's attempt to impede God's plan of redemption by influencing King Saul to kill David, the forefather of the promised Messiah!

The Son of David came not to seek His own, but to do the will of the one who sent Him, to serve, not to be served and gave Himself as a ransom for many, redeeming us from the power of Satan by His sacrificial death on the cross.

God continually calls for justice!

Matt. 12:18–21 NKJV

[18]"Behold! My Servant whom I have chosen, My Beloved in whom My soul is well pleased! I will put My Spirit upon Him, And He will declare justice to the Gentiles.

[19]He will not quarrel nor cry out, Nor will anyone hear His voice in the streets.

[20]A bruised reed He will not break, And smoking flax He will not quench, Till He sends forth justice to victory; [21]And in His name Gentiles will trust."

Deuteronomy 16:19–20 NKJV

[19]You shall not pervert justice; you shall not show partiality, nor take a bribe, for a bribe blinds the eyes of the wise and twists the words of the righteous. [20]You shall follow what is altogether just, that you may live and inherit the land which the Lord your God is giving you.

Psalm 37:27–28 NKJV

[27]Depart from evil, and do good; And dwell forevermore. [28]For the Lord loves justice, And does not forsake His saints; They are preserved forever, But the descendants of the wicked shall be cut off.

Proverbs 16:8 NKJV

[8]Better *is* a little with righteousness, Than vast revenues without justice.

Proverbs 21:3 NKJV

[3]To do righteousness and justice *Is* more acceptable to the Lord than sacrifice.

Isaiah 10:1–2 NKJV

[1]"Woe to those who decree unrighteous decrees, Who write misfortune, *Which* they have prescribed [2]To rob the needy of justice, And to take what is right from the poor of My people, That widows may be their prey, And *that* they may rob the fatherless.

Isaiah 56:1–2 NKJV

[1]Thus says the Lord: "Keep justice, and do righteousness, For My salvation *is* about to come, And My righteousness to be revealed.[2] Blessed *is* the man *who* does this, And the son of man *who* lays hold on it; Who keeps from defiling the Sabbath, And keeps his hand from doing any evil."

Zach. 7:9–10 NKJV

[9]"Thus says the Lord of hosts: 'Execute true justice, Show mercy and compassion Everyone to his brother. [10]Do not oppress the widow or the fatherless, The alien or the poor. Let none of you plan evil in his heart Against his brother.'

Zach 8:16–17 NKJV

[16]These *are* the things you shall do: Speak each man the truth to his neighbor; Give judgment in your gates for truth, justice, and peace; [17]Let none of you think evil in your heart against your neighbor; And do not love a false oath. For all these *are things* that I hate,' Says the Lord."

Micah 6:8 NKJV

[8]He has shown you, O man, what *is* good; And what does the Lord require of you But to do justly, To love mercy, And to walk humbly with your God?

The Nature of Justice, Holman Bible Dictionary

Justice has two major aspects. First, it is the standard by which penalties are assigned for breaking the obligations of the society. Second, justice is the standard by which the advantages of social life are handed out, including material goods, rights of participation, opportunities, and liberties. It is the standard for both punishment and benefits and thus can be spoken of as a plumb line. "I shall use justice as a plumb-line, and righteousness as a plummet" (Isa. 28:17, REB).

Often people think of justice in the Bible only in the first sense as God's wrath on evil. This aspect of justice indeed is present, such as the judgment mentioned in John 3:19. Often more vivid words like "wrath" are used to describe punitive justice (Rom. 1:18).

Justice in the Bible very frequently also deals with benefits. Cultures differ widely in determining the basis by which the benefits are to be justly distributed. For some it is by birth and nobility. For others the basis is might or ability or merit. Or it might simply be whatever is the law or whatever has been established by contracts. The Bible takes another possibility.

Benefits are distributed according to need. Justice then is very close to love and grace. God "executes justice for the orphan and the widow, and ... loves the strangers, providing them food and clothing" (Deut. 10:18, NRSV; compare Hos. 10:12; Isa 30:18).

Various needy groups are the recipients of justice. These groups include widows, orphans, resident aliens (also called "sojourners" or "strangers"), wage earners, the poor, and prisoners, slaves, and the sick (Job 29:12-17; Ps. 146:7-9; Mal. 3:5). Each of these groups has specific needs which keep its members from being able to participate in aspects of the life of their community. Even life itself might be threatened. Justice involves meeting those needs.

The forces which deprive people of what is basic for community life are condemned as oppression (Mic. 2:2; Eccl. 4:1). To oppress is to use power for one's own advantage in depriving others of their basic rights in the community (see Mark 12:40). To do justice is to correct that abuse and to meet those needs (Isa. 1:17). Injustice is depriving others of their basic needs or failing to correct matters when those rights are not met (Jer. 5:28; Job 29:12-17). Injustice is either a sin of commission or of omission.

The content of justice, the benefits which are to be distributed as basic rights in the community, can be identified by observing what is at stake in the passages in which "justice," "righteousness," and "judgment" occur. The needs which are met include land (Ezek. 45:6-9; compare Mic. 2:2; 4:4) and the means to produce from the land, such as draft animals and millstones (Deut. 22:1-4; 24:6).

These productive concerns are basic to securing other essential needs and thus avoiding dependency; thus the millstone is called the "life" of the person (Deut. 24:6). Other needs are those essential for mere physical existence and well being: food (Deut. 10:18; Ps. 146:7), clothing (Deut. 24:13), and shelter (Ps. 68:6; Job 8:6). Job 22:5-9, 23; 24:1-12 decries the injustice of depriving people of each one of these needs, which are material and economic. The equal protection of each person in civil and judicial procedures is represented in the demand for due process (Deut. 16:18-20). Freedom from bondage is comparable to not being "in hunger and thirst, in nakedness and lack of everything" (Deut. 28:48 NRSV).

Justice presupposes God's intention for people to be in community. When people had become poor and weak with respect to the rest of the community, they were to be strengthened so that they could continue to be effective members of the community—living with them and beside them (Lev. 25:35-36). Thus biblical justice restores people to community. By justice those who lacked the power and resources to participate in significant aspects of the community were to be strengthened so that they could. This concern in Leviticus 25 is illustrated by the provision of the year of Jubilee, in which at the end of the fifty year period land is restored to those who had lost it through sale or foreclosure of debts (v. 28). Thus they regained economic power and were brought back into the economic community. Similarly, interest on loans was prohibited (v. 36) as a process which pulled people down, endangering their position in the community.

These legal provisions express a further characteristic of justice. Justice delivers; it does not merely relieve the immediate needs of those in dire straits (Ps. 76:9; Isa. 45:8; 58:11; 62:1-2). Helping the needy means setting them back on their feet, giving a home, leading to prosperity, restoration, ending the oppression (Ps. 68:5-10; 10:15-16; compare 107; 113:7-9). Such thorough justice can be socially disruptive. In the Jubilee year as some receive back lands, others lose recently-acquired additional land.

The advantage to some is a disadvantage to others. In some cases the two aspects of justice come together. In the act of restoration, those who were victims of justice receive benefits while their exploiters are punished (1 Sam 2:7-10; compare Luke 1:51-53; 6:20-26).

The source of justice,
Holman Bible Dictionary

As the sovereign Creator of the universe, God is just (Ps. 99:1-4; Gen. 18:25; Deut. 32:4; Jer. 9:24), particularly as the defender of all the oppressed of the earth (Pss. 76:9; 103:6; Jer. 49:11). Justice thus is universal (Ps. 9:7-9) and applies to each covenant or dispensation. Jesus affirmed for His day the centrality of the Old Testament demand for justice (Matt. 23:23). Justice is the work of the New Testament people of God (Jas. 1:27). God's justice is not a distant external standard. It is the source of all human justice (Prov. 29:26; 2 Chron. 19:6, 9). Justice is grace received and grace shared (2 Cor. 9:8-10).

The most prominent human agent of justice is the ruler. The king receives God's justice and is a channel for it (Ps. 72:1; compare Rom. 13:1-2, 4). There is not a distinction between a personal, voluntary justice and a legal, public justice. The same caring for the needy groups of the society is demanded of the ruler (Ps. 72:4; Ezek. 34:4; Jer. 22:15-16). Such justice was also required of pagan rulers (Dan. 4:27; Prov. 31:8-9).

Justice is also a central demand on all people who bear the name of God. Its claim is so basic that without it other central demands and provisions of God are not acceptable to God. Justice is required to be present with the sacrificial system (Amos 5:21-24; Mic. 6:6-8; Isa. 1:11-17; Matt. 5:23-24), fasting (Isa. 58:1-10), tithing (Matt. 23:23), obedience to the other commandments (Matt. 19:16-21), or the presence of the Temple of God (Jer. 7:1-7).

CHAPTER 5

AUTHORITY
What God Has Given Us through Jesus Christ, Our Redeemer!

To understand and exercise the authority that we have been given by God through Jesus Christ, we need to understand what happened on the cross!

On the cross, Jesus Christ, God's only Son, redeemed us!

Easton's Bible Dictionary

Redeemer
HEB. *goel*; i.e., one charged with the duty of restoring the rights of another and avenging his wrongs (Lev. 25:48–49; Num. 5:8; Ruth 4:1; Job 19:25; Ps. 19:14; 78:35, etc.). This title is peculiarly applied to Christ. He redeems us from all evil by the payment of a ransom. (See REDEMPTION.)

Galatians 3:13–14 NKJV
[13]Christ has redeemed us from the curse of the law, having become a curse for us (for it is written, *"Cursed is everyone who hangs on a tree"*), [14]that the blessing of Abraham might come upon the Gentiles in Christ Jesus, that we might receive the promise of the Spirit through faith.

Galatians 4:4–5 NKJV
⁴But when the fullness of the time had come, God sent forth His Son, born of a woman, born under the law, ⁵to redeem those who were under the law, that we might receive the adoption as sons.

Titus 2:11–14 NKJV
¹¹For the grace of God that brings salvation has appeared to all men, ¹²teaching us that, denying ungodliness and worldly lusts, we should live soberly, righteously, and godly in the present age, ¹³looking for the blessed hope and glorious appearing of our great God and Savior Jesus Christ, ¹⁴who gave Himself for us, that He might redeem us from every lawless deed and purify for Himself *His* own special people, zealous for good works.

1 Tim. 2:3–6 NKJV
³For this *is* good and acceptable in the sight of God our Savior, ⁴who desires all men to be saved and to come to the knowledge of the truth. ⁵For *there is* one God and one Mediator between God and men, *the* Man Christ Jesus, ⁶who gave Himself a ransom for all, to be testified in due time,

Isaiah 53:4–6 NKJV
⁴Surely He has borne our griefs And carried our sorrows; Yet we esteemed Him stricken, Smitten by God, and afflicted. ⁵But He *was* wounded for our transgressions, *He was* bruised for our iniquities; The chastisement for our peace *was* upon Him, And by His stripes we are healed. ⁶All we like sheep have gone astray; We have turned, every one, to his own way; And the Lord has laid on Him the iniquity of us all.

Colossians 1:19–20 NKJV
¹⁹For it pleased *the Father that* in Him all the fullness should dwell, ²⁰and by Him to reconcile all things to Himself, by Him, whether things on earth or things in heaven, having made peace through the blood of His cross.

Romans 5:8–11 NKJV
⁸But God demonstrates His own love toward us, in that while we were still

sinners, Christ died for us. [9]Much more then, having now been justified by His blood, we shall be saved from wrath through Him. [10]For if when we were enemies we were reconciled to God through the death of His Son, much more, having been reconciled, we shall be saved by His life. [11]And not only *that,* but we also rejoice in God through our Lord Jesus Christ, through whom we have now received the reconciliation.

2 Corinthians 5:17–19 NKJV
[17]Therefore, if anyone *is* in Christ, *he is* a new creation; old things have passed away; behold, all things have become new. [18]Now all things *are* of God, who has reconciled us to Himself through Jesus Christ, and has given us the ministry of reconciliation, [19]that is, that God was in Christ reconciling the world to Himself, not imputing their trespasses to them, and has committed to us the word of reconciliation.

Ephesians 1:3–6 NKJV
[3]Blessed *be* the God and Father of our Lord Jesus Christ, who has blessed us with every spiritual blessing in the heavenly *places* in Christ, [4]just as He chose us in Him before the foundation of the world, that we should be holy and without blame before Him in love, [5]having predestined us to adoption as sons by Jesus Christ to Himself, according to the good pleasure of His will, [6]to the praise of the glory of His grace, by which He made us accepted in the Beloved.

Ephesians 2:14–18 NKJV
[14]For He Himself is our peace, who has made both one, and has broken down the middle wall of separation, [15]having abolished in His flesh the enmity, *that is,* the law of commandments *contained* in ordinances, so as to create in Himself one new man *from* the two, *thus* making peace, [16]and that He might reconcile them both to God in one body through the cross, thereby putting to death the enmity. [17]And He came and preached peace to you who were afar off and to those who were near. [18]For through Him we both have access by one Spirit to the Father.

Colossians 1:13–14 NKJV

[13]He has delivered us from the power of darkness and conveyed *us* into the kingdom of the Son of His love, [14]in whom we have redemption through His blood, the forgiveness of sins.

These are just a few of the many wonderful things God has given to us through Jesus Christ, our Redeemer, who restored our rights to us on the cross. I do not believe it is possible to fully understand the depth of the love Jesus Christ had for us when he gave His life on the cross.

All who believe have a <u>Divine Right</u> to all the promises in the Bible because of what Jesus Christ did for us on the cross!

As His disciples, He empowers us by His grace, through the power of the Holy Spirit to walk in the fullness of these promises He made!

The power Jesus Christ used to do mighty works and miracles has been given to all of us who believe because the spirit that raised Christ from the dead now lives within us. That power He has given us is translated from the Greek word Dunamis G1411. Dunamis is the power of God unto salvation (Romans 1:16). The definition of dunamis is in the Appendix Chapter 7 and includes all the words it is translated to with a list of all the verses where it appears in the Bible.

Scriptures identifying authority of this world, whose ruler is Satan, are listed in Chapter 1 of the Appendix. It would be worthwhile to learn them in detail so we have the knowledge to discern and identify them for what they really are, and to refrain from engaging in these kinds of activities. Also, avoid involvement with authorities that practice them to achieve their vision, realizing, they are not acknowledging Jesus Christ as the head of the Church because He tells us in His Word, "It shall not be so among you!"

Conflict with authorities using these worldly principles to achieve their vision is inevitable if we honor the First Commandment. Not because we have chosen to be rebellious, but because the authorities have chosen to violate the boundaries of spiritual authority Jesus Christ established!

In such difficult circumstances, tough decisions have to be made. Will we maintain our faithfulness to God by observing the First Commandment? Or, will we give up our rightful place and give in to those who reject the authority of Jesus Christ and use principles our Lord has forbidden among His people and defined as authority of this world whose ruler is Satan?

In such difficult dilemmas, the great heroes of the Christian Faith we teach our children to model their life after in our Sunday schools listed in chapter 2 are wonderful examples to follow. While they showed respect to the authorities, they refused to submit in the face of judgment when forced to violate the First Commandment!

Chapter 2 of the Appendix lists all the scriptures that define the power and authority (exousia G1849) of God, Jesus Christ, disciples, believers and apostles.

Chapter 4 of the Appendix lists the scriptures that define the power and authority (exousia G1849) of Satan, the Beast, darkness, and the kingdom of darkness.

So, just exactly how do you properly distinguish between the power and authority (exousia G1849) that belongs to God, Jesus Christ, disciples, and New Covenant believers listed in Chapter 2 of the Appendix; and, the power and authority (exousia G1849) scripture attributes to Satan, the devil, the Beast, and the kingdom of darkness listed in Chapter 4 of the Appendix?

It can seem overwhelming, but God has given us the Holy Spirit who leads us into all truth. Jesus Christ has promised, if we continue in His Word, we will know the truth and the truth will set us free.

It essential that we learn the difference so we are not deceived and mistakenly use or submit to and support authorities who use the power and authority (exousia G1849) scripture attributes to the enemy who is Satan—instead of—the power and authority (exousia G1849) that belongs to God, which He has imparted to us who believe through His only Son, Jesus Christ!

If we don't get this right, it could have tragic eternal consequences! Not only for ourselves, but those around us who are affected by it!

It's like being given the keys to the car. It is the driver's responsible to learn how to drive it and educate themselves about the rules of the road. If the driver doesn't learn the rules of the road or doesn't follow the rules of the road, it can be very harmful, even catastrophe, involving innocent people.

So it is with authority!

God had given authority to Adam at creation, Satan stole it to pursue his own ambitions, and Jesus Christ gave Himself on the cross to restore our rights to it! It is our responsibility to educate ourselves how to accurately use it to overcome all the power and authority of the enemy so we can serve and edify one another in love to the glory of God.

Satan will tempt us to use this authority for our own gain as he tempted Jesus Christ in the wilderness. Let's not be like Satan who used it for his own ambitions and end up facing the same condemnation he is facing!

We must be vigilant and alert against the devil's devious attacks, as they *will* come. But Jesus Christ has overcome him and has given us power and authority (exousia G1849) over all the power and authority (exousia G1849) of Satan! We don't have to earn it. We have it now! It was given as a free gift because of His great love for us! We can freely use it now! Today! Against all the powers of hell that come against us! We need to use it against every thought that exalts itself above the Most High! Against every evil force that tries to separate us from God and each other! It is not a battle that we might win if we fight hard and long enough! It's a battle already won on the cross—where Jesus Christ shed His innocent blood for us. So, let us walk by faith in the victory He has given us by exercising our rights to the power and authority He restored to us on the cross!

The following scriptures can help us recognize those who have learned to overcome Satan's influence by exercising their rights to the power and authority (exousia G1849) Jesus Christ restored to us on the cross. And those under the influence of the power and authority (exousia G1849) scripture attributes to Satan, darkness, and the kingdom of darkness caused by the fall of Adam.

Not that we condemn them; Jesus Christ came not to condemn (John 3:17), but that we might have life. Furthermore Romans 8:1 NKJV tells us, "There is therefore now no condemnation for them

that are in Christ Jesus, who walk not according to the flesh but according the Spirit." So how could condemnation rightfully come out of us if we truly are in Christ Jesus and walk according the spirit?

Instead we share the Good News of the Gospel, the redemption from the power and authority (exousia G1849) of Satan Jesus Christ gave us on the cross! And be a light in darkness, turning them from the power of darkness to light! In addition to being an example, we help and encourage them to understand and utilize the fullness of their rights to power and authority (exousia G1849), the miraculous power (dunamis G1411) and the glorious hope of the New Covenant believer they have been given as adopted children in God's kingdom of marvelous light!

1 John 3:10–12 NKJV

[10]In this the children of God and the children of the devil are manifest: Whoever does not practice righteousness is not of God, nor *is* he who does not love his brother. [11]For this is the message that you heard from the beginning, that we should love one another, [12]not as Cain *who* was of the wicked one and murdered his brother. And why did he murder him? Because his works were evil and his brother's righteous.

Galatians 5:19–25 NKJV

[19]Now the works of the flesh are evident, which are: adultery, fornication, uncleanness, lewdness, [20]idolatry, sorcery, hatred, contentions, jealousies, outbursts of wrath, selfish ambitions, dissensions, heresies, [21]envy, murders, drunkenness, revelries, and the like; of which I tell you beforehand, just as I also told *you* in time past, that those who practice such things will not inherit the kingdom of God.

[22]But the fruit of the Spirit is love, joy, peace, longsuffering, kindness, goodness, faithfulness, [23]gentleness, self-control. Against such there is no law. [24]And those *who are* Christ's have crucified the flesh with its passions and desires. [25]If we live in the Spirit, let us also walk in the Spirit.

James 3:13–18 NKJV

[13]Who *is* wise and understanding among you? Let him show by good conduct *that* his works *are done* in the meekness of wisdom. [14]But if you have bitter envy and self-seeking in your hearts, do not boast and lie against the truth. [15]This wisdom does not descend from above, but *is* earthly, sensual, demonic. [16]For where envy and self-seeking *exist,* confusion and every evil thing *are* there. [17]But the wisdom that is from above is first pure, then peaceable, gentle, willing to yield, full of mercy and good fruits, without partiality and without hypocrisy. [18]Now the fruit of righteousness is sown in peace by those who make peace.

1 John 4:7–11 NKJV

[7]Beloved, let us love one another, for love is of God; and everyone who loves is born of God and knows God. [8]He who does not love does not know God, for God is love. [9]In this the love of God was manifested toward us, that God has sent His only begotten Son into the world, that we might live through Him. [10]In this is love, not that we loved God, but that He loved us and sent His Son *to be* the propitiation for our sins. [11]Beloved, if God so loved us, we also ought to love one another.

1 John 4:20–21 NKJV

[20]If someone says, "I love God," and hates his brother, he is a liar; for he who does not love his brother whom he has seen, how can he love God whom he has not seen? [21]And this commandment we have from Him: that he who loves God *must* love his brother also.

John 15:9–17 NKJV

[9]"As the Father loved Me, I also have loved you; abide in My love. [10]If you keep My commandments, you will abide in My love, just as I have kept My Father's commandments and abide in His love.
[11]"These things I have spoken to you, that My joy may remain in you, and *that* your joy may be full. [12]This is My commandment, that you love one another as I have loved you. [13]Greater love has no one than this, than to lay down one's life for his friends. [14]You are My friends if you do

whatever I command you. [15]No longer do I call you servants, for a servant does not know what his master is doing; but I have called you friends, for all things that I heard from My Father I have made known to you. [16]You did not choose Me, but I chose you and appointed you that you should go and bear fruit, and *that* your fruit should remain, that whatever you ask the Father in My name He may give you. [17]These things I command you, that you love one another.

Romans 13:8–10 NKJV

[8]Owe no one anything except to love one another, for he who loves another has fulfilled the law. [9]For the commandments, *"You shall not commit adultery," "You shall not murder," "You shall not steal," "You shall not bear false witness," "You shall not covet,"* and if *there is* any other commandment, are *all* summed up in this saying, namely, *"You shall love your neighbor as yourself."* [10]Love does no harm to a neighbor; therefore love *is* the fulfillment of the law.

1 John 3:14 NKJV

[14]We know that we have passed from death to life, because we love the brethren. He who does not love *his* brother abides in death.

1 John 3:16–19 NKJV

[16]By this we know love, because He laid down His life for us. And we also ought to lay down *our* lives for the brethren. [17]But whoever has this world's goods, and sees his brother in need, and shuts up his heart from him, how does the love of God abide in him?
[18]My little children, let us not love in word or in tongue, but in deed and in truth. [19]And by this we know that we are of the truth, and shall assure our hearts before Him.

John 10:7–16 NKJV

[7]Then Jesus said to them again, "Most assuredly, I say to you, I am the door of the sheep. [8]All who *ever* came before Me are thieves and robbers, but the sheep did not hear them. [9]I am the door. If anyone enters by Me, he will be saved, and will go in and out and find pasture. [10]The thief does not

come except to steal, and to kill, and to destroy. I have come that they may have life, and that they may have *it* more abundantly. [11]"I am the good shepherd. The good shepherd gives His life for the sheep. [12]But a hireling, *he who is* not the shepherd, one who does not own the sheep, sees the wolf coming and leaves the sheep and flees; and the wolf catches the sheep and scatters them. [13]The hireling flees because he is a hireling and does not care about the sheep. [14]I am the good shepherd; and I know My *sheep,* and am known by My own. [15]As the Father knows Me, even so I know the Father; and I lay down My life for the sheep. [16]And other sheep I have which are not of this fold; them also I must bring, and they will hear My voice; and there will be one flock *and* one shepherd.

So, let's not be deceived!

Luke 7:21 NKJV

[21]"Not everyone who says to Me, 'Lord, Lord,' shall enter the kingdom of heaven, but he who does the will of My Father in heaven."

John 6:40 NKJV

[40]And this is the will of Him who sent Me, that everyone who sees the Son and believes in Him may have everlasting life; and I will raise him up at the last day."

John 13:34–35 NKJV

[34]A new commandment I give to you, that you love one another; as I have loved you, that you also love one another. [35]By this all will know that you are My disciples, if you have love for one another."

John 3:36 NKJV

[36]He who believes in the Son has everlasting life; and he who does not believe the Son shall not see life, but the wrath of God abides on him.

1 John 3:23 NKJV

[23]And this is His commandment: that we should believe on the name of His Son Jesus Christ and love one another, as He gave us commandment.

Appendix

Authority in the New Testament

King James Bible
Authority (ies) appears 36 times in 33 verses. It's translated from seven Greek words:

New King James Bible
Authority (ies) appears 73 times in 67 verses. It's translated from twelve Greek words:

New Living Translation
Authority (ies) appears 126 times in 113 verses

Greek words in the New Testament authority is translated from:

	King James Bible	New King James Bible
G1849 exousia	29 times	53 times
G2715 katexousiazo	2 times	2 times
G1850 exousiazo	1 time	3 times
G1413 dunastes	1 time	1 time
G5247 huperuche	1 time	1 time
G831 authenteo	1 time	1 time
G2003 epitage	1 time	1 time

G1683 emautou/emauto/emauton	3 times
G1438 heautou	2 times
G758 archon	1 time
G1415 dunatos	1 time
G2963 kuriotes	2 times

Exousia G1849

Exousia, the Greek word most often translated to authority, is used to define the power and authority of God, Jesus Christ, apostles, disciples, believers, Satan, the devil, the Beast, and the kingdom of darkness.

Exousia appears 103 times in 93 verses;
it's translated as follows in Chapters 2–4:

	King James Bible	New King James Bible
Authority (ies)	29 times	53 times
Power (s)	69 times	38 times
Right (s)	2 times	8 times
Liberty	1 time	1 time
Jurisdiction	1 time	1 time
Strength	1 time	
Control		1 time

Order of study

* First, the word that is being studied
* Second, Strong's number and Greek definition
* Third, Thayer's number and Greek definition
* Fourth, list of the English words it is translated to with all the verses where that word appears in the Bible
* That's followed with the scriptures in three translations every time that word appears for easy comparison

58

*   The King James Version with the Strong's number and translation of the word being studied underlined, in bold print
*   The New King James Version
*   The New Living Translation
*   Only the verse where the Greek word appears is used. You may need to look up the verses before and after it to get a complete understanding of the passage.

CHAPTER 1

AUTHORITY
Of This WORLD As
Defined by Jesus Christ

Jesus Christ used four Greek words in three verses to define authority of this world that do not belong among His people. Here are those four words, every time they appear in the Bible!

Matt. 20:25 KJV
²⁵But Jesus G2424 called G4341 them unto him, and said G2036, Ye know G1492 that the princes G758 of the Gentiles G1484 **exercise G2634 dominion G2634** over them, and they that are great G3171 **exercise G2715 authority G2715** upon them.

Mark 10:42 KJV
⁴²But Jesus G2424 called G4341 them to him, and saith G3004 unto them, Ye know G1492 that they which are accounted G1380 to rule G757 over the Gentiles G1484 **exercise G2634 lordship G2634** over them; and their great G3173 ones **exercise G2715 authority G2715** upon them.

Luke 22:25 KJV
[25]And he said G2036 unto them, The kings G935 of the Gentiles G1484 **exercise G2961 lordship G2961** over them; and they that **exercise G1850 authority G1850** upon them are called G2564 benefactors G2110.

Katakurieuo

G2634
katakurieuo
kat-ak-oo-ree-yoo'-o
From G2596 and G2961; to *lord against*; that is, *control, subjugate:*—exercise dominion over (lordship), be lord over, overcome.

G2634
katakurieuo
Thayer Definition:
1) to bring under one's power, to subject one's self, to subdue, master
2) to hold in subjection, to be master of, exercise lordship over
Part of Speech: verb
A Related Word by Thayer's/Strong's Number: from G2596 and G2961
Total KJV Occurrences: 8
exercise, 2
Matt 20:25; Mark 10:42
lords, 2
1 Pet. 5:3; Rev. 17:14
dominion, 1
Matt. 20:25
lordship, 1
Mark 10:42
over, 1
1 Pet. 5:3
overcame, 1
Acts 19:16

Matt. 20:25

KJV

²⁵But Jesus G2424 called G4341 them unto him, and said G2036, Ye know G1492 that the princes G758 of the Gentiles G1484 **exercise G2634 dominion G2634** over them, and they that are great G3171 exercise G2715 authority G2715 upon them.

NKJV

²⁵But Jesus called them to *Himself* and said, "You know that the rulers of the Gentiles lord it over them, and those who are great exercise authority over them.

NLT

²⁵But Jesus called them together and said, "You know that the rulers in this world lord it over their people, and officials flaunt their authority over those under them.

Mark 10:42

KJV

⁴²But Jesus G2424 called G4341 them to him, and saith G3004 unto them, Ye know G1492 that they which are accounted G1380 to rule G757 over the Gentiles G1484 **exercise G2634 lordship G2634** over them; and their great G3173 ones exercise G2715 authority G2715 upon them.

NKJV

⁴²But Jesus called them to *Himself* and said to them, "You know that those who are considered rulers over the Gentiles lord it over them, and their great ones exercise authority over them.

NLT

⁴²So Jesus called them together and said, "You know that the rulers in this world lord it over their people, and officials flaunt their authority over those under them.

Acts 19:16

KJV

¹⁶And the man G444 in whom G3739 the evil G4190 spirit G4151 was leaped G2177 on G1909 them, and **overcame G2634** them, and prevailed G2480 against G2596 them, so G5620 that they fled G1628 out of that house G3624 naked G1131 and wounded G5135.

NKJV

¹⁶Then the man in whom the evil spirit was leaped on them, overpowered them, and prevailed against them, so that they fled out of that house naked and wounded.

NLT

¹⁶Then the man with the evil spirit leaped on them, overpowered them, and attacked them with such violence that they fled from the house, naked and battered.

1 Peter 5:3

KJV

³Neither G3366 as being **lords G2634 over G2634** God's G2316 heritage G2819, but being G1096 ensamples G5179 to the flock G4168.

NKJV

³nor as being lords over those entrusted to you, but being examples to the flock;

NLT

³Don't lord it over the people assigned to your care, but lead them by your own good example.

Revelations 17:14

KJV

¹⁴These G3778 shall make G4170 war G4170 with the Lamb G721, and the Lamb G721 shall overcome G3528 them: for he is Lord G2962 **of lords G2634**, and King G935 of kings G935: and they that are with him are called G2822, and chosen G1588, and faithful G4103.

NKJV

¹⁴These will make war with the Lamb, and the Lamb will overcome them, for He is Lord of lords and King of kings; and those *who are* with Him *are* called, chosen, and faithful."

NLT

¹⁴Together they will go to war against the Lamb, but the Lamb will defeat them because he is Lord of all lords and King of all kings. And his called and chosen and faithful ones will be with him."

Katexousiazo

G2715
katexousiazo
kat-ex-oo-see-ad'-zo
From G2596 and G1850; to *have* (*wield*) *full privilege over:*—exercise authority.

G2715
katexousiazo
Thayer Definition:
1) to exercise authority, wield power
Part of Speech: verb
A Related Word by Thayer's/Strong's Number: from **G2596** and **G1850**
Total KJV Occurrences: 4
authority, 2
Matt. 20:24–25 (2); Mark 10:42
exercise, 2
Matt. 20:25; Mark 10:42

Matthew 20:25
KJV
[25]But Jesus G2424 called G4341 them unto him, and said G2036, Ye know G1492 that the princes G758 of the Gentiles G1484 exercise G2634 dominion G2634 over them, and they that are great G3171 **exercise G2715 authority G2715** upon them.
NKJV
[25]But Jesus called them to *Himself* and said, "You know that the rulers of the Gentiles lord it over them, and those who are great exercise authority over them.
NLT
[25]But Jesus called them together and said, "You know that the rulers in this world lord it over their people, and officials flaunt their authority over those under them.

Mark 10:42

KJV

⁴²But Jesus G2424 called G4341 them to him, and saith G3004 unto them, Ye know G1492 that they which are accounted G1380 to rule G757 over the Gentiles G1484 exercise G2634 lordship G2634 over them; and their great G3173 ones **exercise G2715 authority G2715** upon them.

NKJV

⁴²But Jesus called them to *Himself* and said to them, "You know that those who are considered rulers over the Gentiles lord it over them, and their great ones exercise authority over them.

NLT

⁴²So Jesus called them together and said, "You know that the rulers in this world lord it over their people, and officials flaunt their authority over those under them.

Kurieuo

G2961

kurieuo

koo-ree-yoo'-o

From G2962; to *rule:*—have dominion over, lord, be lord of, exercise lordship over.

G2961

kurieuo

Thayer Definition:

1) to be lord of, to rule, have dominion over

2) of things and forces

2a) to exercise influence upon, to have power over

Part of Speech: verb

A Related Word by Thayer's/Strong's Number: from **G2962**

Total KJV Occurrences: 8

dominion, 4

Rom 6:9, Rom 6:14, Rom 7:1, 2 Cor 1:24

exercise, 1

Luke 22:24-25 (2)

lord, 1
Rom 14:9
lords, 1
1 Tim 6:15
lordship, 1
Luke 22:25

Luke 22:25
KJV
²⁵And he said G2036 unto them, The kings G935 of the Gentiles G1484 **exercise G2961 lordship G2961** over them; and they that exercise G1850 authority G1850 upon them are called G2564 benefactors G2110.
NKJV
²⁵And He said to them, "The kings of the Gentiles exercise lordship over them, and those who exercise authority over them are called 'benefactors.'
NLT
²⁵Jesus told them, "In this world the kings and great men lord it over their people, yet they are called 'friends of the people.'

Romans 6:9
KJV
⁹Knowing G1492 that Christ G5547 being raised G1453 from the dead G3498 dieth G599 no G3765 more G2089; death G2288 hath no G3765 more G3765 **dominion G2961** over him.
NKJV
⁹knowing that Christ, having been raised from the dead, dies no more. Death no longer has dominion over Him.
NLT
⁹We are sure of this because Christ was raised from the dead, and he will never die again. Death no longer has any power over him.

Romans 6:14
KJV
¹⁴For sin G266 shall not have **dominion G2961** over you: for ye are not under G5259 the law G3551, but under G5259 grace G5485.

NKJV

¹⁴For sin shall not have dominion over you, for you are not under law but under grace.

NLT

¹⁴Sin is no longer your master, for you no longer live under the requirements of the law. Instead, you live under the freedom of God's grace.

Romans 7:1

KJV

¹Know G50 ye not, brethren G80, (for I speak G2980 to them that know G1097 the law G3551) how that the law G3551 hath **dominion G2961** over a man G444 as long G5550 as he liveth G2198?

NKJV

¹Or do you not know, brethren (for I speak to those who know the law), that the law has dominion over a man as long as he lives?

NLT

¹Now, dear brothers and sisters you who are familiar with the law—don't you know that the law applies only while a person is living?

Romans 14:9

KJV

⁹For to this G5124 end Christ G5547 both G2532 died G599, and rose G450, and revived G326, that he might be **Lord G2961** both G2532 of the dead G3498 and living G2198.

NKJV

⁹For to this end Christ died and rose and lived again, that He might be Lord of both the dead and the living.

NLT

⁹Christ died and rose again for this very purpose—to be Lord both of the living and of the dead.

2 Corinthians 1:24

KJV

²⁴Not for that we have **dominion G2961** over your G5216 faith G4102, but are helpers G4904 of your G5216 joy G5479: for by faith G4102 ye stand G2476.

NKJV

²⁴Not that we have dominion over your faith, but are fellow workers for your joy; for by faith you stand.

NLT

²⁴But that does not mean we want to dominate you by telling you how to put your faith into practice. We want to work together with you so you will be full of joy, for it is by your own faith that you stand firm.

1 Timothy 6:15

KJV

¹⁵Which G3739 in his times G5550 he shall show G1166, who G3588 is the blessed G3107 and only G3441 Potentate G1413, the King G935 of kings G936, and Lord G2962 of **lords G2961;**

NKJV

¹⁵which He will manifest in His own time, *He who is* the blessed and only Potentate, the King of kings and Lord of lords,

NLT

¹⁵For at just the right time Christ will be revealed from heaven by the blessed and only almighty God, the King of all kings and Lord of all lords.

Exousiazo

G1850

exousiazo

ex-oo-see-ad'-zo

From G1849; to *control:*—exercise authority upon, bring under the (have) power of.

G1850

exousiazo

Thayer Definition:

1) to have power or authority, use power

1a) to be master of any one, exercise authority over one

1b) to be master of the body

1b1) to have full and entire authority over the body

1b2) to hold the body subject to one's will

1c) to be brought under the power of anyone
Part of Speech: verb
A Related Word by Thayer's/Strong's Number: from **G1849**
Total KJV Occurrences: 6
power, 3
1 Cor. 6:12; 1 Cor. 7:4 (2)
authority, 1
Luke 22:25
brought, 1
1 Cor. 6:12
exercise, 1
Luke 22:25

Luke 22:25
KJV
²⁵And he said G2036 unto them, The kings G935 of the Gentiles G1484 exercise G2961 lordship G2961 over them; and they that **exercise G1850 authority G1850** upon them are called G2564 benefactors G2110.
NKJV
²⁵And He said to them, "The kings of the Gentiles exercise lordship over them, and those who exercise authority over them are called 'benefactors.'
NLT
²⁵Jesus told them, "In this world the kings and great men lord it over their people, yet they are called 'friends of the people.'

1 Corinthians 6:12
KJV
¹²All G3956 things are lawful G1832 unto me, but all G3956 things are not expedient G4851: all G3956 things are lawful G1832 for me, but I will not be **brought G1850** under G5259 **the power G1850** of any G5100.
NKJV
¹²All things are lawful for me, but all things are not helpful. All things are lawful for me, but I will not be brought under the power of any.

NLT

[12]You say, "I am allowed to do anything"—but not everything is good for you. And even though "I am allowed to do anything," I must not become a slave to anything.

1 Corinthians 7:4

KJV

[4]The wife G1135 hath not **power G1850** of her own G2398 body G4983, but the husband G435: and likewise G3668 also G2532 the husband G435 hath not **power G1850** of his own G2398 body G4983, but the wife G1135.

NKJV

[4]The wife does not have authority over her own body, but the husband *does*. And likewise the husband does not have authority over his own body, but the wife *does*.

NLT

[4]The wife gives authority over her body to her husband, and the husband gives authority over his body to his wife.

AUTHORITY
God's Kingdom of Light

In the following scriptures,
Exousia identifies the following:

The power and authority of God (6)
The power and authority of Christ/Son of Man (18)
The power and authority of disciples (5)
The power, authority and rights of servants/believers (11)
The power, authority and rights of apostles (11)
The power and authority of angels (2)
The power of two witnesses (2)

Exousia G1849
Greek word most often translated to authority
Greek definitions from
Strong's and Thayer's dictionaries

G1849
εξουσία
exousia
ex-oo-see'-ah

From G1832 (in the sense of *ability*); *privilege*, that is, (subjectively) *force*, *capacity*, *competency*, *freedom*, or (objectively) *mastery* (concretely *magistrate*, *superhuman*, *potentate*, *token of control*), delegated *influence:*— authority, jurisdiction, liberty, power, right, strength.

G1849

εξουσία

exousia

Thayer's Definition:

1) power of choice, liberty of doing as one pleases

1a) leave or permission

2) physical and mental power

2a) the ability or strength with which one is endued, which he either possesses or exercises

3) the power of authority (influence) and of right (privilege)

4) the power of rule or government (the power of him whose will and commands must be submitted to by others and obeyed)

4a) universally

4a1) authority over mankind

4b) specifically

4b1) the power of judicial decisions

4b2) of authority to manage domestic affairs

4c) metonymically

4c1) a thing subject to authority or rule

4c1a) jurisdiction

4c2) one who possesses authority

4c2a) a ruler, a human magistrate

4c2b) the leading and more powerful among created beings superior to man, spiritual potentates

4d) a sign of the husband's authority over his wife

4d1) the veil with which propriety required a women to cover herself

4e) the sign of regal authority, a crown

Part of Speech: noun feminine

A Related Word by Thayer's/Strong's Number: from **G1832** (in the sense of ability)

Total KJV Occurrences 103

power, 61

Matt. 9:6; Matt. 9:8; Matt. 10:1; Matt. 28:18; Mark 2:10; Mark 3:15; Mark 6:7; Luke 4:6; Luke 4:32; Luke 5:24; Luke 10:19; Luke 12:5; Luke 22:53; John 1:12; John 10:18 (2); John 17:2; John 19:10–11 (3); Acts 1:7; Acts 5:4; Acts 8:19; Acts 26:18; Rom. 9:21; Rom. 13:1–3 (3); 1 Cor. 7:37; 1 Cor. 9:4–6 (3); 1 Cor. 9:12 (2); 1 Cor. 9:18; 1 Cor. 11:10; 2 Cor. 13:10; Eph. 1:21; Eph. 2:2; Col. 1:13; Col. 2:10; 2 Thess. 3:9; Rev. 2:25–26 (2); Rev. 6:8; Rev. 9:3 (2); Rev. 9:10; Rev. 9:19; Rev. 11:6 (2); Rev. 12:10; Rev. 13:4–5 (2); Rev. 13:7; Rev. 13:12; Rev. 14:18; Rev. 16:9; Rev. 17:12; Rev. 18:1; Rev. 20:6

authority, 28

Matt. 7:29; Matt. 8:9; Matt. 21:23–24 (3); Matt. 21:27; Mark 1:22; Mark 11:27–29 (4); Mark 13:33–34 (2); Luke 4:36; Luke 7:8; Luke 9:1; Luke 19:17; Luke 20:2 (2); Luke 20:8; Luke 20:20; John 5:27; Acts 9:14; Acts 26:10; Acts 26:12; 1 Cor. 15:24; 2 Cor. 10:8; Rev 13:2

powers, 8

Luke 12:11; Rom. 13:1 (2); Eph. 3:10; Eph. 6:12; Col. 1:16; Col. 2:15, Titus 3:1

right, 2

Heb. 13:10; Rev. 22:14

authorities, 1

1 Pet. 3:22

jurisdiction, 1

Luke 23:7

liberty, 1

1 Cor. 8:9

strength, 1

Rev. 17:13

The power and authority of God (6)

Luke 12:5

KJV

⁵But I will forewarn G5263 you whom G5101 ye shall fear G5399: Fear G5399 him, which after G3326 he hath killed G615 hath G2192 **power G1849** to cast G1685 into G1519 hell G1067; yea G3483, I say G3004 unto you, Fear G5399 him.

NKJV

⁵But I will show you whom you should fear: Fear Him who, after He has killed, has power to cast into hell; yes, I say to you, fear Him!

NLT

⁵But I'll tell you whom to fear. Fear God, who has the power to kill you and then throw you into hell. Yes, he's the one to fear.

John 19:11

KJV

¹¹Jesus G2424 answered G611, Thou couldest have G2192 no G3756 **power G1849** at all G3762 against G2596 me, except G1508 it were given G1325 thee from above G509: therefore G1223–G5124 he that delivered G3860 me unto thee hath G2192 the greater G3187 sin G266.

NKJV

¹¹Jesus answered, "You could have no power at all against Me unless it had been given you from above. Therefore the one who delivered Me to you has the greater sin."

NLT

¹¹Then Jesus said, "You would have no power over me at all unless it were given to you from above. So the one who handed me over to you has the greater sin."

Acts 1:7

KJV

⁷And he said G2036 unto them, It is not for you to know G1097 the times

G5550 or G2228 the seasons G2540, which G3739 the Father G3962 hath put G5087 in his own G2398 **power G1849.**

NKJV

[7]And He said to them, "It is not for you to know times or seasons which the Father has put in His own authority.

NLT

[7]He replied, "The Father alone has the authority to set those dates and times, and they are not for you to know.

Romans 9:21

KJV

[21]Hath G2192 not the potter G2763 **power G1849** over the clay G4081, of the same G846 lump G5445 to make G4160 one vessel G4632 unto honour G5092, and another G3739 unto dishonor G819?

NKJV

[21]Does not the potter have power over the clay, from the same lump to make one vessel for honor and another for dishonor?

NLT

[21]When a potter makes jars out of clay, doesn't he have a right to use the same lump of clay to make one jar for decoration and another to throw garbage into?

Jude 1:25

KJV

[25]To the only G3441 wise G4680 God G2316 our Saviour G4990, be glory G1391 and majesty G3172, dominion G2904 and **power G1849**, both G2532 now G3568 and for ever G3956–G165. Amen G281.

NKJV

[25]To God our Savior, Who alone is wise, *Be* glory and majesty, Dominion and power, Both now and forever. Amen.

NLT

[25]All glory to him who alone is God, our Savior through Jesus Christ our Lord. All glory, majesty, power, and authority are his before all time, and in the present, and beyond all time! Amen.

Revelations 16:9

KJV

⁹And men G444 were scorched G2739 with great G3173 heat G2738, and blasphemed G987 the name G3686 of God G2316, which G3588 hath G2192 **power G1849** over G1909 these G5025 plagues G4127: and they repented G3340 not to give G1325 him glory G1391.

NKJV

⁹And men were scorched with great heat, and they blasphemed the name of God who has power over these plagues; and they did not repent and give Him glory.

NLT

⁹Everyone was burned by this blast of heat, and they cursed the name of God, who had control over all these plagues. They did not repent of their sins and turn to God and give him glory.

The power and authority of Christ/Son of Man (18)

Matt. 7:29

KJV

²⁹For he taught G2258–G1321 them as one having G2192 **authority G1849**, and not as the scribes G1122.

NKJV

²⁹for He taught them as one having authority, and not as the scribes.

NLT

²⁹for he taught with real authority—quite unlike their teachers of religious law.

Matt. 9:6

KJV

⁶But that ye may know G1492 that the Son G5207 of man G444 hath G2192 **power G1849** on G1909 earth G1093 to forgive G863 sins G266, (then G5119 saith G3004 he to the sick G3885 of the palsy G3885,) Arise G1453, take G142 up thy bed G2825, and go G5217 unto thine G4675 house G3624.

NKJV

⁶But that you may know that the Son of Man has power on earth to forgive sins"—then He said to the paralytic, "Arise, take up your bed, and go to your house."

NLT

⁶So I will prove to you that the Son of Man has the authority on earth to forgive sins." Then Jesus turned to the paralyzed man and said, "Stand up, pick up your mat, and go home!"

Matt 9:8

KJV

⁸But when the multitude G3793 saw G1492 it, they marvelled G2296, and glorified G1392 God G2316, which G3588 had given G1325 such G5108 **power G1849** unto men G444.

NKJV

⁸Now when the multitudes saw *it,* they marveled and glorified God, who had given such power to men.

NLT

⁸Fear swept through the crowd as they saw this happen. And they praised God for sending a man with such great authority.

Matt 28:18

KJV

¹⁸And Jesus G2424 came G4334 and spake G2980 unto them, saying G3004, All G3956 **power G1849** is given G1325 unto me in heaven G3772 and in earth G1093.

NKJV

¹⁸And Jesus came and spoke to them, saying, "All authority has been given to Me in heaven and on earth.

NLT

¹⁸Jesus came and told his disciples, "I have been given all authority in heaven and on earth.

Mark 1:22

KJV

²²And they were astonished G1605 at G1909 his doctrine G1322: for he taught G2258–G1321 them as one that had G2192 **authority G1849**, and not as the scribes G1122.

NKJV

²²And they were astonished at His teaching, for He taught them as one having authority, and not as the scribes.

NLT

²²The people were amazed at his teaching, for he taught with real authority—quite unlike the teachers of religious law.

Mark 1:27

KJV

²⁷And they were all G3956 amazed G2284, insomuch G5620 that they questioned G4802 among G4314 themselves G848, saying G3004, What G5101 thing is this G3778? What G5101 new G2537 doctrine G1322 is this G5124? for with **authority G1849** commandeth G2004 he even G2532 the unclean G169 spirits G4151, and they do obey G5219 him.

NKJV

²⁷Then they were all amazed, so that they questioned among themselves, saying, "What is this? What new doctrine *is* this? For with authority He commands even the unclean spirits, and they obey Him."

NLT

²⁷Amazement gripped the audience, and they began to discuss what had happened. "What sort of new teaching is this?" they asked excitedly. "It has such authority! Even evil spirits obey his orders!"

Mark 2:10

KJV

¹⁰But that ye may know G1492 that the Son G5207 of man G444 hath G2192 **power G1849** on G1909 earth G1093 to forgive G863 sins G266, (he saith G3004 to the sick G3885 of the palsy G3885,)

NKJV

[10]But that you may know that the Son of Man has power on earth to forgive sins"—He said to the paralytic,

NLT

[10]So I will prove to you that the Son of Man has the authority on earth to forgive sins." Then Jesus turned to the paralyzed man and said,

Luke 4:32

KJV

[32]And they were astonished G1605 at G1909 his doctrine G1322: for his word G3056 was with **power G1849.**

NKJV

[32]And they were astonished at His teaching, for His word was with authority.

NLT

[32]There, too, the people were amazed at his teaching, for he spoke with authority

Luke 4:36

KJV

[36]And they were all G3956 amazed G1096–G2285, and spake G4814 among G4314 themselves G240, saying G3004, What G5101 a word G3056 is this G3778! for with **authority G1849** and power G1411 he commandeth G2004 the unclean G169 spirits G4151, and they come G1831 out.

NKJV

[36]Then they were all amazed and spoke among themselves, saying, "What a word this *is!* For with authority and power He commands the unclean spirits, and they come out.

NLT

[36]Amazed, the people exclaimed, "What authority and power this man's words possess! Even evil spirits obey him, and they flee at his command!

Luke 5:24

KJV

²⁴But that ye may know G1492 that the Son G5207 of man G444 hath G2192 **power G1849** upon earth G1093 to forgive G863 sins G266, (he said G2036 unto the sick G3885 of the palsy G3886,) I say G3004 unto thee, Arise G1453, and take G142 up thy couch G2826, and go G4198 into G1519 thine G4675 house G3624.

NKJV

²⁴But that you may know that the Son of Man has power on earth to forgive sins"—He said to the man who was paralyzed, "I say to you, arise, take up your bed, and go to your house."

NLT

²⁴So I will prove to you that the Son of Man has the authority on earth to forgive sins." Then Jesus turned to the paralyzed man and said, "Stand up, pick up your mat, and go home!"

John 5:27

KJV

²⁷And hath given G1325 him **authority G1849** to execute G4160 judgment G2920 also G2532, because G3754 he is the Son G5207 of man G444.

NKJV

²⁷and has given Him authority to execute judgment also, because He is the Son of Man.

NLT

²⁷And he has given him authority to judge everyone because he is the Son of Man.

John 10:18

KJV

¹⁸No G3762 man G3762 taketh G142 it from me, but I lay G5087 it down of myself G1683. I have G2192 **power G1849** to lay G5087 it down, and I have G2192 **power G1849** to take G2983 it again G3825. This G5026 commandment G1785 have G2192 I received G2983 of my Father G3962.

NKJV

[18]No one takes it from Me, but I lay it down of Myself. I have power to lay it down, and I have power to take it again. This command I have received from My Father."

NLT

[18]No one can take my life from me. I sacrifice it voluntarily. For I have the authority to lay it down when I want to and also to take it up again. For this is what my Father has commanded."

John 17:2

KJV

[2]As thou hast given G1325 him **power G1849** over all G3956 flesh G4561, that he should give G1325 eternal G166 life G2222 to as many as thou hast given G1325 him.

NKJV

[2]as You have given Him authority over all flesh, that He should give eternal life to as many as You have given Him.

NLT

[2]For you have given him authority over everyone. He gives eternal life to each one you have given him.

1 Corinthians 15:24

KJV

[24]Then G1534 cometh the end G5056, when G3752 he shall have delivered G3860 up the kingdom G932 to God G2316, even G2532 the Father G3962; when G3752 he shall have put G2673 down G2673 all G3956 rule G746 and all G3956 **authority G1849** and power G1411.

NKJV

[24]Then *comes* the end, when He delivers the kingdom to God the Father, when He puts an end to all rule and all authority and power.

NLT

[24]After that the end will come, when he will turn the Kingdom over to God the Father, having destroyed every ruler and authority and power.

Ephesians 1:21

KJV

²¹Far G5231 above G5231 all G3956 principality G746, and **power G1849**, and might G1411, and dominion G2963, and every G3956 name G3686 that is named G3687, not only G3440 in this G3588 world G165, but also G2532 in that which is to come G3195:

NKJV

²¹far above all principality and power and might and dominion, and every name that is named, not only in this age but also in that which is to come.

NLT

²¹Now he is far above any ruler or authority or power or leader or anything else—not only in this world but also in the world to come.

Colossians 1:16

KJV

¹⁶For by him were all G3956 things created G2936, that are in heaven G3772, and that are in earth G1093, visible G3707 and invisible G517, whether G1535 they be thrones G2362, or G1535 dominions G2963, or G1535 principalities G746, or G1535 **powers G1849**: all G3956 things were created G2936 by him, and for him:

NKJV

¹⁶For by Him all things were created that are in heaven and that are on earth, visible and invisible, whether thrones or dominions or principalities or powers. All things were created through Him and for Him.

NLT

¹⁶ for through him God created everything
in the heavenly realms and on earth.
He made the things we can see
and the things we can't see—
such as thrones, kingdoms, rulers, and authorities in the unseen world.
Everything was created through him and for him.

1 Peter 3:22

KJV

²²Who G3739 is gone G4198 into G1519 heaven G3772, and is on G1722 the right G1188 hand of God G2316; angels G32 and **authorities G1849** and powers G1411 being made G5293 subject G5293 unto him.

NKJV

²²who has gone into heaven and is at the right hand of God, angels and authorities and powers having been made subject to Him.

NLT

²²Now Christ has gone to heaven. He is seated in the place of honor next to God, and all the angels and authorities and powers accept his authority.

Revelations 12:10

KJV

¹⁰And I heard G191 a loud G3173 voice G5456 saying G3004 in heaven G3772, Now G737 is come G1096 salvation G4991, and strength G1411, and the kingdom G932 of our God G2316, and the **power G1849** of his Christ G5547: for the accuser G2725 of our brethren G80 is cast G2598 down G2598, which G3588 accused G2723 them before G1799 our God G2316 day G2250 and night G3571.

NKJV

¹⁰Then I heard a loud voice saying in heaven, "Now salvation, and strength, and the kingdom of our God, and the power of His Christ have come, for the accuser of our brethren, who accused them before our God day and night, has been cast down.

NLT

¹⁰Then I heard a loud voice shouting across the heavens,
"It has come at last—
salvation and power
and the Kingdom of our God,
and the authority of his Christ
For the accuser of our brothers and sisters
has been thrown down to earth—
the one who accuses them
before our God day and night.

The power and authority of disciples (5)

Matthew 10:1

KJV

¹And when he had called G4341 unto him his twelve G1427 disciples G3101, he gave G1325 them **power G1849** against unclean G169 spirits G4151, to cast G1544 them out, and to heal G2323 all G3956 manner of sickness G3554 and all G3956 manner of disease G3119

NKJV

¹And when He had called His twelve disciples to *Him,* He gave them power *over* unclean spirits, to cast them out, and to heal all kinds of sickness and all kinds of disease.

NLT

¹Jesus called his twelve disciples together and gave them authority to cast out evil spirits and to heal every kind of disease and illness.

Mark 3:15

KJV

¹⁵And to have G2192 **power G1849** to heal G2323 sicknesses G3554, and to cast G1544 out devils G1140:

NKJV

¹⁵and to have power to heal sicknesses and to cast out demons:

NLT

¹⁵giving them authority to cast out demons.

Mark 6:7

KJV

⁷And he called G4341 unto him the twelve G1427, and began G756 to send G649 them forth G1614 by two G1417 and two G1417; and gave G1325 them **power G1849** over unclean G169 spirits G4151;

NKJV

⁷And He called the twelve to *Himself,* and began to send them out two *by* two, and gave them power over unclean spirits.

NLT

⁷And he called his twelve disciples together and began sending them out two by two, giving them authority to cast out evil spirits.

Luke 9:1

KJV

¹Then G1161 he called G4779 his twelve G1427 disciples G3101 together G4779, and gave G1325 them power G1411 and **authority G1849** over G1909 all G3956 devils G1140, and to cure G2323 diseases G3554
NKJV.

¹Then He called His twelve disciples together and gave them power and authority over all demons, and to cure diseases.

NLT

¹One day Jesus called together his twelve disciples and gave them power and authority to cast out demons and to heal all diseases.

Luke 10:19

KJV

¹⁹Behold G2400, I give G1325 unto you **power G1849** to tread G3961 on G1883 serpents G3789 and scorpions G4651, and over G1909 all G3956 the power G1411 of the enemy G2190: and nothing G3762 shall by any G3364 means G3364 hurt G91 you.

NKJV

¹⁹Behold, I give you the authority to trample on serpents and scorpions, and over all the power of the enemy, and nothing shall by any means hurt you.

NLT,

¹⁹Look, I have given you authority over all the power of the enemy, and you can walk among snakes and scorpions and crush them. Nothing will injure you.

The power, authority and rights of servants/ believers (11)

John 1:12

KJV

¹²But as many G3745 as received G2983 him, to them gave G1325 he

power G1849 to become G1096 the sons G5043 of God G2316, even to them that believe G4100 on G1519 his name G3686:

NKJV

[12]But as many as received Him, to them He gave the right to become children of God, to those who believe in His name:

NLT

[12]But to all who believed him and accepted him, he gave the right to become children of God.

Mark 13:34

KJV

[34]For the Son of man is as a man G444 taking a far journey G590, who left G863 his house G3614, and gave G1325 **authority G1849** to his servants G1401, and to every G1538 man his work G2041, and commanded G1781 the porter G2377 to watch G1127.

NKJV

[34]*It is* like a man going to a far country, who left his house and gave authority to his servants, and to each his work, and commanded the doorkeeper to watch.

NLT

[34]"The coming of the Son of Man can be illustrated by the story of a man going on a long trip. When he left home, he gave each of his slaves instructions about the work they were to do, and he told the gatekeeper to watch for his return.

Luke 19:17

KJV

[17]And he said G2036 unto him, Well G2095, thou good G18 servant G1401: because G3754 thou hast been G1096 faithful G4103 in a very G1646 little G1646, have G2192 thou **authority G1849** over G1883 ten G1176 cities G4172.

NKJV

[17]And he said to him, 'Well *done,* good servant; because you were faithful in a very little, have authority over ten cities.'

NLT

17"'Well done!' the king exclaimed. 'You are a good servant. You have been faithful with the little I entrusted to you, so you will be governor of ten cities as your reward.'

Acts 5:4

KJV

4Whiles it remained G3306, was it not thine G4671 own? and after it was sold G4097, was it not in thine G3588–G4674 own **power G1849**? Why G5101 hast thou conceived G5087 this G5124 thing G4229 in thine G4675 heart G2588? thou hast not lied G5574 unto men G444, but unto God G2316.

NKJV

4While it remained, was it not your own? And after it was sold, was it not in your own control? Why have you conceived this thing in your heart? You have not lied to men but to God."

NLT

4The property was yours to sell or not sell, as you wished. And after selling it, the money was also yours to give away. How could you do a thing like this? You weren't lying to us but to God!"

1 Corinthians 7:37

KJV

37Nevertheless G1161 he that standeth G2476 stedfast G1476 in his heart G2588, having G2192 no G3361 necessity G318, but hath G2192 **power G1849** over G4012 his own G2398 will G2307, and hath so G5124 decreed G2919 in his heart G2588 that he will keep G5083 his virgin G3933, doeth G4160 well G2573.

NKJV

37Nevertheless he who stands steadfast in his heart, having no necessity, but has power over his own will, and has so determined in his heart that he will keep his virgin, does well.

NLT

37But if he has decided firmly not to marry and there is no urgency and he can control his passion, he does well not to marry.

1 Corinthians 8:9

KJV

⁹But take heed G991 lest G3381 by any G3381 means G4458 this G3778 **liberty G1849** of yours G5216 become G1096 a stumblingblock G4348 to them that are weak G770.

NKJV

⁹But beware lest somehow this liberty of yours become a stumbling block to those who are weak.

NLT

⁹But you must be careful so that your freedom does not cause others with a weaker conscience to stumble.

1 Corinthians 11:10

KJV

¹⁰For this G5124 cause G1223 ought G3784 the woman G1135 to have G2192 **power G1849** on G1909 her head G2776 because G1223 of the angels G32.

NKJV

¹⁰For this reason the woman ought to have *a symbol of* authority on *her* head, because of the angels.

NLT

¹⁰For this reason, and because the angels are watching, a woman should wear a covering on her head to show she is under authority.

Colossians 2:10

KJV

¹⁰And ye are complete G4137 in him, which G3739 is the head G2776 of all G3956 principality G746 and **power G1849:**

NKJV

¹⁰and you are complete in Him, who is the head of all principality and power.

NLT

¹⁰So you also are complete through your union with Christ, who is the head over every ruler and authority.

Revelations 2:26

KJV

²⁶And he that overcometh G3528, and keepeth G5083 my works G2041 unto the end G5056, to him will I give G1325 **power G1849** over G1909 the nations G1484:

NKJV

²⁶And he who overcomes, and keeps My works until the end, to him I will give power over the nations—

NLT

²⁶To all who are victorious, who obey me to the very end,

To them I will give authority over all the nations.

Revelations 20:6

KJV

⁶Blessed G3107 and holy G40 is he that hath G2192 part G3313 in the first G4413 resurrection G386: on G1909 such G5130 the second G1208 death G2288 hath G2192 no G3756 **power G1849,** but they shall be priests G2409 of God G2316 and of Christ G5547, and shall reign G936 with him a thousand G5507 years G2094.

NKJV

⁶Blessed and holy *is* he who has part in the first resurrection. Over such the second death has no power, but they shall be priests of God and of Christ, and shall reign with Him a thousand years.

NLT

⁶Blessed and holy are those who share in the first resurrection. For them the second death holds no power, but they will be priests of God and of Christ and will reign with him a thousand years.

Revelations 22:14

KJV

¹⁴Blessed G3107 are they that do G4160 his commandments G1785, that they may have G2071 **right G1849** to the tree G3586 of life G2222, and may enter G1525 in through the gates G4440 into G1519 the city G4172.

NKJV

¹⁴Blessed *are* those who do His commandments, that they may have the right to the tree of life, and may enter through the gates into the city.

NLT

¹⁴Blessed are those who wash their robes. They will be permitted to enter through the gates of the city and eat the fruit from the tree of life.

The power, authority and rights of apostles (11)

Acts 8:19

KJV

¹⁹Saying G3004, Give G1325 me also G2504 this G5026 **power G1849,** that on G2007 whomsoever G3739–G302 I lay G2007 hands G5495, he may receive G2983 the Holy G40 Ghost G4151.

NKJV

¹⁹saying, "Give me this power also, that anyone on whom I lay hands may receive the Holy Spirit."

NLT

¹⁹"Let me have this power, too," he exclaimed, "so that when I lay my hands on people, they will receive the Holy Spirit!"

1 Corinthians 9:4–6

KJV

⁴Have G2192 we not **power G1849** to eat G5315 and to drink G4095?
⁵Have G2192 we not **power G1849** to lead G4013 about G4013 a sister G79, a wife G1135, as well G2532 as other G3062 apostles G652, and as the brethren G80 of the Lord G2962, and Cephas G2786? ⁶Or G2228 I only G3441 and Barnabas G921, have G2192 not we **power G1849** to forbear G3361 working G2038?

NKJV

⁴Do we have no right to eat and drink? ⁵Do we have no right to take along a believing wife, as *do* also the other apostles, the brothers of the Lord, and Cephas? ⁶Or *is it* only Barnabas and I *who* have no right to refrain from working?

NLT

[4]Don't we have the right to live in your homes and share your meals? [5]Don't we have the right to bring a Christian wife with us as the other disciples and the Lord's brothers do, and as Peter does? [6]Or is it only Barnabas and I who have to work to support ourselves?

1 Corinthians 9:12

KJV

[12]If G1487 others G243 be partakers G3348 of this G3588 **power G1849** over you, are not we rather G3123? Nevertheless G235 we have G2192 not used G5530 this G5026 **power G1849**; but suffer G4722 all G3956 things, lest G2443–G3361 we should hinder G5100–G1464–G1325 the gospel G2098 of Christ G5547.

NKJV

[12]If others are partakers of *this* right over you, *are* we not even more? Nevertheless we have not used this right, but endure all things lest we hinder the gospel of Christ.

NLT

[12]If you support others who preach to you, shouldn't we have an even greater right to be supported? But we have never used this right. We would rather put up with anything than be an obstacle to the Good News about Christ.

1 Corinthians 9:18

KJV

[18]What G5101 is my reward G3408 then G3767? Verily that, when I preach G2097 the gospel G2097, I may make G5087 the gospel G2098 of Christ G5547 without G77 charge G77, that I abuse G2710 not my **power G1849** in the gospel G2098.

NKJV

[18]What is my reward then? That when I preach the gospel, I may present the gospel of Christ without charge, that I may not abuse my authority in the gospel.

NLT

[18]What then is my pay? It is the opportunity to preach the Good News without charging anyone. That's why I never demand my rights when I preach the Good News.

2 Corinthians 10:8

KJV

[8]For though G1437 I should boast G2744 somewhat G5100 more G4055 of our **authority G1849**, which G3739 the Lord G2962 hath given G1325 us for edification G3619, and not for your G5216 destruction G2506, I should not be ashamed G153:

NKJV

[8]For even if I should boast somewhat more about our authority, which the Lord gave us for edification and not for your destruction, I shall not be ashamed—

NLT

[8]I may seem to be boasting too much about the authority given to us by the Lord. But our authority builds you up; it doesn't tear you down. So I will not be ashamed of using my authority.

2 Corinthians 13:10

KJV

[10]Therefore G1223–G5124 I write G1125 these G5023 things being absent G548, lest G2443–G3361 being present G3918 I should use G5530 sharpness G664, according G2596 to the **power G1849** which G3739 the Lord G2962 hath given G1325 me to edification G3619, and not to destruction G2506.

NKJV

[10]Therefore I write these things being absent, lest being present I should use sharpness, according to the authority which the Lord has given me for edification and not for destruction.

NLT

[10]I am writing this to you before I come, hoping that I won't need to deal severely with you when I do come. For I want to use the authority the Lord has given me to strengthen you, not to tear you down.

2 Thessalonians 3:9

KJV

⁹Not because G3754 we have G2192 not **power G1849**, but to make G1325 ourselves G1438 an ensample G5179 unto you to follow G3401 us.

NKJV

⁹not because we do not have authority, but to make ourselves an example of how you should follow us.

NLT

⁹We certainly had the right to ask you to feed us, but we wanted to give you an example to follow.

Hebrews 13:10

KJV

¹⁰We have G2192 an altar G2379, whereof G1537–G3739 they have G2192 no G3756 **right G1849** to eat G5315 which serve G3000 the tabernacle G4633.

NKJV

¹⁰We have an altar from which those who serve the tabernacle have no right to eat.

NLT

¹⁰We have an altar from which the priests in the Tabernacle have no right to eat.

The power and authority of angels (2)

Revelations 14:18

KJV

¹⁸And another G243 angel G32 came G1831 out from the altar G2379, which had G2192 **power G1849** over G1909 fire G4442; and cried G5455 with a loud G3173 cry G2906 to him that had G2192 the sharp G3691 sickle G1407, saying G3004, Thrust G3992 in thy sharp G3691 sickle G1407, and gather G5166 the clusters G1009 of the vine G288 of the earth G1093; for her grapes G4718 are fully ripe G187.

NKJV

¹⁸And another angel came out from the altar, who had power over fire, and

he cried with a loud cry to him who had the sharp sickle, saying, "Thrust in your sharp sickle and gather the clusters of the vine of the earth, for her grapes are fully ripe."
NLT
[18]Then another angel, who had power to destroy with fire, came from the altar. He shouted to the angel with the sharp sickle, "Swing your sickle now to gather the clusters of grapes from the vines of the earth, for they are ripe for judgment."

Revelations 18:1
KJV
[1]And after G3326 these G5023 things I saw G1492 another G243 angel G32 come G2597 down G2597 from heaven G3772, having G2192 great G3173 **power G1849;** and the earth G1093 was lightened G5461 with his glory G1391.
NKJV
[1]After these things I saw another angel coming down from heaven, having great authority, and the earth was illuminated with his glory.
NLT
[1]After all this I saw another angel come down from heaven with great authority, and the earth grew bright with his splendor.

The power of witnesses (2)

Revelations 11:6
KJV
[6]These G3778 have G2192 **power G1849** to shut G2808 heaven G3772, that it rain G1026–G5205 not in the days G2250 of their prophecy G4394: and have G2192 **power G1849** over G1909 waters G5204 to turn G4762 them to blood G129, and to smite G3960 the earth G1093 with all G3956 plagues G4127, as often G3740 as they will G2309.
NKJV
[6]These have power to shut heaven, so that no rain falls in the days of their prophecy; and they have power over waters to turn them to blood, and to strike the earth with all plagues, as often as they desire.

NLT

[6]They have power to shut the sky so that no rain will fall for as long as they prophesy. And they have the power to turn the rivers and oceans into blood, and to strike the earth with every kind of plague as often as they wish.

CHAPTER 3

AUTHORITY
Civil Authorities

In the followings scriptures,
Exousia G1849 identifies Civil Authorities.

The power and authority of governments, governor (10)
The power and jurisdiction of Herod and Pilate (3)
The authority of the centurion 2)
The questions the chief priests and elders had about Jesus' authority (11)
The authority Saul had from the chief priests and elders to kill all who call on the name (3)

The power and authority of governments,
governor (10)

Luke 12:11
KJV
¹¹And when G3752 they bring G4374 you unto the synagogues G4864, and unto magistrates G746, and **powers G1849**, take ye no G3361 thought G3309 how G4459 or G2228 what G5101 thing ye shall answer G626, or G2228 what G5101 ye shall say G2036:
NKJV
¹¹"Now when they bring you to the synagogues and magistrates and

authorities, do not worry about how or what you should answer, or what you should say.

NLT

¹¹"And when you are brought to trial in the synagogues and before rulers and authorities, don't worry about how to defend yourself or what to say.

Luke 20:20

KJV

²⁰And they watched G3906 him, and sent G649 forth G649 spies G1455, which should feign G5271 themselves G1438 just G1342 men, that they might take G1949 hold G1949 of his words G3056, that so G1519 they might deliver G3860 him unto the power G746 and **authority G1849** of the governor G2230.

NKJV

²⁰So they watched *Him,* and sent spies who pretended to be righteous, that they might seize on His words, in order to deliver Him to the power and the authority of the governor.

NLT

²⁰Watching for their opportunity, the leaders sent spies pretending to be honest men. They tried to get Jesus to say something that could be reported to the Roman governor so he would arrest Jesus.

Romans 13:1–3

KJV

¹Let every G3956 soul G5590 be subject G5293 unto the higher G5242 **powers G1849**. For there is no G3756 **power G1849** but of God G2316: the **powers G1849** that be are ordained G5021 of God G2316.
²Whosoever G3588 therefore G5620 resisteth G498 the **power G1849**, resisteth G436 the ordinance G1296 of God G2316: and they that resist G436 shall receive G2983 to themselves G1438 damnation G2917.
³For rulers G758 are not a terror G5401 to good G18 works G2041, but to the evil G2556. Wilt G2309 thou then G1161 not be afraid G5399 of the **power G1849?** Do G4160 that which is good G18, and thou shalt have G2192 praise G1868 of the same G846:

NKJV

[1]Let every soul be subject to the governing authorities. For there is no authority except from God, and the authorities that exist are appointed by God. [2]Therefore whoever resists the authority resists the ordinance of God, and those who resist will bring judgment on themselves. [3]For rulers are not a terror to good works, but to evil. Do you want to be unafraid of the authority? Do what is good, and you will have praise from the same.

NLT

[1]Everyone must submit to governing authorities. For all authority comes from God, and those in positions of authority have been placed there by God. [2]So anyone who rebels against authority is rebelling against what God has instituted, and they will be punished. [3]For the authorities do not strike fear in people who are doing right, but in those who are doing wrong. Would you like to live without fear of the authorities? Do what is right, and they will honor you.

Ephesians 3:10

KJV

[10]To the intent G2443 that now G3568 unto the principalities G746 and **powers G1849** in heavenly G2032 places might be known G1107 by the church G1577 the manifold G4182 wisdom G4678 of God G2316,

NKJV

[10]to the intent that now the manifold wisdom of God might be made known by the church to the principalities and powers in the heavenly *places,*

NLT

[10]God's purpose in all this was to use the church to display his wisdom in its rich variety to all the unseen rulers and authorities in the heavenly places.

Titus 3:1

KJV

[1]Put G5279 them in mind G5279 to be subject G5293 to principalities G746 and **powers G1849**, to obey G3980 magistrates G3980, to be ready G2092 to every G3956 good G18 work G2041,

NKJV

¹Remind them to be subject to rulers and authorities, to obey, to be ready for every good work,

NLT

¹Remind the believers to submit to the government and its officers. They should be obedient, always ready to do what is good.

1 Peter 3:22

KJV

²²Who G3739 is gone G4198 into G1519 heaven G3772, and is on G1722 the right G1188 hand of God G2316; angels G32 and **authorities G1849** and powers G1411 being made G5293 subject G5293 unto him.

NKJV

²²who has gone into heaven and is at the right hand of God, angels and authorities and powers having been made subject to Him.

NLT

²²Now Christ has gone to heaven. He is seated in the place of honor next to God, and all the angels and authorities and powers accept his authority.

The power and jurisdiction Herod and Pilate (3)

Luke 23:7

KJV

⁷And as soon as he knew G1921 that he belonged G1510 unto Herod's G2264 **jurisdiction G1849,** he sent G375 him to Herod G2264, who himself G846 also G2532 was at G1722 Jerusalem G2414 at G1722 that time G2250.

NKJV

⁷And as soon as he knew that He belonged to Herod's jurisdiction, he sent Him to Herod, who was also in Jerusalem at that time.

NLT

⁷When they said that he was, Pilate sent him to Herod Antipas, because Galilee was under Herod's jurisdiction, and Herod happened to be in Jerusalem at the time.

John 19:10

KJV

¹⁰Then G3767 saith G3004 Pilate G4091 unto him, Speakest G2980 thou not unto me? Knowest G1492 thou not that I have G2192 **power G1849** to crucify G4717 thee, and have G2192 **power G1849** to release G630 thee?

NKJV

¹⁰Then Pilate said to Him, "Are You not speaking to me? Do You not know that I have power to crucify You, and power to release You?"

NLT

¹⁰"Why don't you talk to me?" Pilate demanded. "Don't you realize that I have the power to release you or crucify you?"

The authority of the centurion (2)

Matthew 8:9

KJV

⁹For I am G1510 a man G444 under G5259 **authority G1849**, having G2192 soldiers G4757 under G5259 me: and I say G3004 to this G5129 man, Go G4198, and he goeth G4198; and to another G243, Come G2064, and he cometh G2064; and to my servant G1401, Do G4160 this G5124, and he doeth G4160 it.

NKJV

⁹For I also am a man under authority, having soldiers under me. And I say to this *one*, 'Go,' and he goes; and to another, 'Come,' and he comes; and to my servant, 'Do this,' and he does *it.*"

NLT

⁹I know this because I am under the authority of my superior officers, and I have authority over my soldiers. I only need to say, 'Go,' and they go, or 'Come,' and they come. And if I say to my slaves, 'Do this,' they do it."

Luke 7:8

KJV

⁸For I also G2532 am G1510 a man G444 set G5021 under G5259 **authority G1849,** having G2192 under G5259 me soldiers G4757, and I say G3004 unto one G5129, Go G4198, and he goeth G4198; and to another

G243, Come G2064, and he cometh G2064; and to my servant G1401, Do G4160 this G5124, and he doeth G4238 it.

NKJV

[8]For I also am a man placed under authority, having soldiers under me. And I say to one, 'Go,' and he goes; and to another, 'Come,' and he comes; and to my servant, 'Do this,' and he does *it.*"

NLT

[8]I know this because I am under the authority of my superior officers, and I have authority over my soldiers. I only need to say, 'Go,' and they go, or 'Come,' and they come. And if I say to my slaves, 'Do this,' they do it."

The questions the chief priests and elders had about Jesus' authority (11)

Matthew 21:23–24

KJV

[23]And when he was come G2064 into G1519 the temple G2411, the chief G749 priests G749 and the elders G4245 of the people G2992 came G4334 unto him as he was teaching G1321, and said G3004, By what G4169 **authority G1849** doest G4160 thou these G5023 things? and who G5101 gave G1325 thee this G5026 **authority G1849**?

[24]And Jesus G2424 answered G611 and said G2036 unto them, I also G2504 will ask G2065 you one G1520 thing G3056, which G3739 if G1437 ye tell G2036 me, I in like G2504 wise will tell G2046 you by what G4169 **authority G1849** I do G4160 these G5023 things.

NKJV

[23]Now when He came into the temple, the chief priests and the elders of the people confronted Him as He was teaching, and said, "By what authority are You doing these things? And who gave You this authority?"

[24]But Jesus answered and said to them, "I also will ask you one thing, which if you tell Me, I likewise will tell you by what authority I do these things:

NLT

[23]When Jesus returned to the Temple and began teaching, the leading priests and elders came up to him. They demanded, "By what authority are you doing all these things? Who gave you the right?"

²⁴"I'll tell you by what authority I do these things if you answer one question," Jesus replied.

Matthew 21:27

KJV

²⁷And they answered G611 Jesus G2424, and said G2036, We cannot G3756–G1492 tell G1492. And he said G5346 unto them, Neither G3761 tell G3004 I you by what G4169 **authority G1849** I do G4160 these G5023 things.

NKJV

²⁷So they answered Jesus and said, "We do not know."

And He said to them, "Neither will I tell you by what authority I do these things.

NLT

²⁷So they finally replied, "We don't know."

And Jesus responded, "Then I won't tell you by what authority I do these things.

Mark 11:28–29

KJV

²⁸And say G3004 unto him, By what G4169 **authority G1849** doest G4160 thou these G5023 things? and who G5101 gave G1325 thee this G5026 **authority G1849** to do G4160 these G5023 things?

²⁹And Jesus G2424 answered G611 and said G2036 unto them, I will also G2504 ask G1905 of you one G1520 question G3056, and answer G611 me, and I will tell G2046 you by what G4169 **authority G1849** I do G4160 these G5023 things.

NKJV

²⁸And they said to Him, "By what authority are You doing these things? And who gave You this authority to do these things?"

²⁹But Jesus answered and said to them, "I also will ask you one question; then answer Me, and I will tell you by what authority I do these things:

NLT

²⁸They demanded, "By what authority are you doing all these things? Who gave you the right to do them?"

[29]"I'll tell you by what authority I do these things if you answer one question," Jesus replied.

Mark 11:33
KJV
[33]And they answered G611 and said G3004 unto Jesus G2424, We cannot G3756–G1492 tell G1492. And Jesus G2424 answering G611 saith G3004 unto them, Neither G3761 do G4160 I tell G3004 you by what G4169 **authority G1849** I do these G5023 things.
NKJV
[33]So they answered and said to Jesus, "We do not know."
And Jesus answered and said to them, "Neither will I tell you by what authority I do these things."
NLT
[33]So they finally replied, "We don't know."
And Jesus responded, "Then I won't tell you by what authority I do these things."

Luke 20:2
KJV
[2]And spake G2036 unto him, saying G3004, Tell G2036 us, by what G4169 **authority G1849** doest G4160 thou these G5023 things? Or G2228 who G5101 is he that gave G1325 thee this G5026 **authority G1849?**
NKJV
[2]and spoke to Him, saying, "Tell us, by what authority are You doing these things? Or who is he who gave You this authority?"
NLT
[2]They demanded, "By what authority are you doing all these things? Who gave you the right?"

Luke 20:8
KJV
[8]And Jesus G2424 said G2036 unto them, Neither G3761 tell G3004 I you by what G4169 **authority G1849** I do G4160 these G5023 things.

NKJV
[8]And Jesus said to them, "Neither will I tell you by what authority I do these things."
NLT
[8]And Jesus responded, "Then I won't tell you by what authority I do these things."

The authority Saul had from chief priests and elders to kill all who call on the name (3)

Acts 9:14
KJV
[14]And here G5602 he hath G2192 **authority G1849** from the chief G749 priests G749 to bind G1210 all G3956 that call G1941 on thy name G3686.
NKJV
[14]And here he has authority from the chief priests to bind all who call on Your name."
NLT
[14]And he is authorized by the leading priests to arrest everyone who calls upon your name."

Acts 26:10
KJV
[10]Which G3739 thing I also G2532 did in Jerusalem G2414: and many G4183 of the saints G40 did G4160 I shut G2623 up in prison G5438, having received G2983 **authority G1849** from the chief G749 priests G749; and when they were put G337 to death G337, I gave G2702 my voice G5586 against G2702 them.
NKJV
[10]This I also did in Jerusalem, and many of the saints I shut up in prison, having received authority from the chief priests; and when they were put to death, I cast my vote against *them.*
NLT
[10]Indeed, I did just that in Jerusalem. Authorized by the leading priests, I caused many believers there to be sent to prison. And I cast my vote against them when they were condemned to death.

Acts 26:12

KJV

[12]Whereupon G1722–G3739 as I went G4198 to Damascus G1154 with **authority G1849** and commission G2011 from the chief G749 priests G749,

NKJV

[12]"While thus occupied, as I journeyed to Damascus with authority and commission from the chief priests,

NLT

[12]"One day I was on such a mission to Damascus, armed with the authority and commission of the leading priests.

CHAPTER 4

AUTHORITY
The Dark Side

In the following Scriptures, Exousia G1849 identifies

The power and authority of the devil, Satan, darkness, and the kingdom of darkness (7)
The power and authority of the Beast and the Dragon (7)
The power of the pale horse, locusts, scorpions, and serpents (5)

The power and authority of the devil, Satan, darkness and rulers of darkness (7)

Luke 4:6
KJV
⁶And the devil G1228 said G2036 unto him, All G537 this G5026 **power G1849** will I give G1325 thee, and the glory G1391 of them: for that is delivered G3860 unto me; and to whomsoever G3739–G1437 I will G2309 I give G1325 it.
NKJV
⁶And the devil said to Him, "All this authority I will give You, and their glory; for *this* has been delivered to me, and I give it to whomever I wish.

NLT

⁶"I will give you the glory of these kingdoms and authority over them," the devil said, "because they are mine to give to anyone I please.

Luke 22:53

KJV

⁵³When I was daily G2596–G2250 with you in the temple G2411, ye stretched G1614 forth G1614 no G3756 hands G5495 against G1909 me: but this G3778 is your G5216 hour G5610, and the **power G1849** of darkness G4655.

NKJV

⁵³When I was with you daily in the temple, you did not try to seize Me. But this is your hour, and the power of darkness."

NLT

⁵³Why didn't you arrest me in the Temple? I was there every day. But this is your moment, the time when the power of darkness reigns."

Acts 26:18

KJV

¹⁸To open G455 their eyes G3788, and to turn G1994 them from darkness G4655 to light G5457, and from the **power G1849** of Satan G4567 unto God G2316, that they may receive G2983 forgiveness G859 of sins G266, and inheritance G2819 among G1722 them which are sanctified G37 by faith G4102 that is in me.

NKJV

¹⁸to open their eyes, *in order* to turn *them* from darkness to light, and *from* the power of Satan to God, that they may receive forgiveness of sins and an inheritance among those who are sanctified by faith in Me.'

NLT

¹⁸to open their eyes, so they may turn from darkness to light and from the power of Satan to God. Then they will receive forgiveness for their sins and be given a place among God's people, who are set apart by faith in me.'

Ephesians 2:2

KJV

²Wherein G1722–G3757 in time G4218 past ye walked G4043 according G2596 to the course G165 of this G5127 world G2889, according G2596 to the prince G758 of the **power G1849** of the air G109, the spirit G4151 that now G3568 worketh G1754 in the children G5207 of disobedience G543:

NKJV

²in which you once walked according to the course of this world, according to the prince of the power of the air, the spirit who now works in the sons of disobedience,

NLT

²You used to live in sin, just like the rest of the world, obeying the devil—the commander of the powers in the unseen world. He is the spirit at work in the hearts of those who refuse to obey God.

Ephesians 6:12

KJV

¹²For we wrestle G2076–G3823 not against G4314 flesh G4561 and blood G129, but against G4314 principalities G746, against G4314 **powers G1849**, against G4314 the rulers G2888 of the darkness G4655 of this G5127 world G165, against G4314 spiritual G4152 wickedness G4189 in high G2032 places.

NKJV

¹²For we do not wrestle against flesh and blood, but against principalities, against powers, against the rulers of the darkness of this age, against spiritual *hosts* of wickedness in the heavenly *places.*

NLT

¹²For we are not fighting against flesh-and-blood enemies, but against evil rulers and authorities of the unseen world, against mighty powers in this dark world, and against evil spirits in the heavenly places.

Colossians 1:13

KJV

¹³Who G3739 hath delivered G4506 us from the **power G1849** of darkness

G4655, and hath translated G3179 us into G1519 the kingdom G932 of his dear G26 Son G5207:

NKJV

[13]He has delivered us from the power of darkness and conveyed *us* into the kingdom of the Son of His love,

NLT

[13]For he has rescued us from the kingdom of darkness and transferred us into the Kingdom of his dear Son,

Colossians 2:15

KJV

[15]And having spoiled G554 principalities G746 and **powers G1849**, he made G1165 a show G1165 of them openly G1722–G3954, triumphing G2358 over them in it.

NKJV

[15]Having disarmed principalities and powers, He made a public spectacle of them, triumphing over them in it.

NLT

[15]In this way, he disarmed the spiritual rulers and authorities. He shamed them publicly by his victory over them on the cross.

The power and authority of the Beast and Dragon (7)

Revelations 13:2

[2]And the beast G2342 which G3739 I saw G1492 was like G3664 unto a leopard G3917, and his feet G4228 were as the feet G4228 of a bear G715, and his mouth G4750 as the mouth G4750 of a lion G3023: and the dragon G1404 gave G1325 him his power G1411, and his seat G2362, and great G3173 **authority G1849.**

NKJV

[2]Now the beast which I saw was like a leopard, his feet were like *the feet of* a bear, and his mouth like the mouth of a lion. The dragon gave him his power, his throne, and great authority.

NLT

[2]This beast looked like a leopard, but it had the feet of a bear and the mouth

of a lion! And the dragon gave the beast his own power and throne and great authority.

Revelations 13:4–5

KJV

⁴And they worshipped G4352 the dragon G1404 which G3739 gave G1325 **power G1849** unto the beast G2342: and they worshipped G4352 the beast G2342, saying G3004, Who G5101 is like G3664 unto the beast G2342? Who G5101 is able G1410 to make G4170 war G4170 with him? ⁵And there was given G1325 unto him a mouth G4750 speaking G2980 great G3173 things and blasphemies G988; and **power G1849** was given G1325 unto him to continue G4160 forty G5062 and two G1417 months G3376.

NKJV

⁴So they worshiped the dragon who gave authority to the beast; and they worshiped the beast, saying, "Who *is* like the beast? Who is able to make war with him?"

⁵And he was given a mouth speaking great things and blasphemies, and he was given authority to continue for forty-two months.

NLT

⁴They worshiped the dragon for giving the beast such power, and they also worshiped the beast. "Who is as great as the beast?" they exclaimed. "Who is able to fight against him?"

⁵Then the beast was allowed to speak great blasphemies against God. And he was given authority to do whatever he wanted for forty-two months.

Revelations 13:7

KJV

⁷And it was given G1325 unto him to make G4160 war G4171 with the saints G40, and to overcome G3528 them: and **power G1849** was given G1325 him over G1909 all G3956 kindreds G5443, and tongues G1100, and nations G1484.

NKJV

⁷It was granted to him to make war with the saints and to overcome them. And authority was given him over every tribe, tongue, and nation.

NLT

⁷And the beast was allowed to wage war against God's holy people and to conquer them. And he was given authority to rule over every tribe and people and language and nation.

Revelations 13:12

KJV

¹²And he exerciseth G4160 all G3956 the **power G1849** of the first G4413 beast G2342 before G1799 him, and causeth G4160 the earth G1093 and them which dwell G2730 therein G1722–G846 to worship G4352 the first G4413 beast G2342, whose G3739 deadly G2288 wound G4127 was healed G2323.

NKJV

¹²And he exercises all the authority of the first beast in his presence, and causes the earth and those who dwell in it to worship the first beast, whose deadly wound was healed.

NLT

¹²He exercised all the authority of the first beast. And he required all the earth and its people to worship the first beast, whose fatal wound had been healed.

Revelations 17:12–13

KJV

¹²And the ten G1176 horns G2768 which G3739 thou sawest G1492 are ten G1176 kings G935, which G3748 have received G2983 no G3768 kingdom G932 as yet G3768; but receive G2983 **power G1849** as kings G935 one G3391 hour G5610 with the beast G2342.
¹³These G3778 have G2192 one G3391 mind G1106, and shall give G1239 their power G1411 and **strength G1849** unto the beast G2342.

NKJV

¹²"The ten horns which you saw are ten kings who have received no kingdom as yet, but they receive authority for one hour as kings with the beast.
¹³These are of one mind, and they will give their power and authority to the beast.

NLT

¹²The ten horns of the beast are ten kings who have not yet risen to power. They will be appointed to their kingdoms for one brief moment to reign with the beast. ¹³They will all agree to give him their power and authority.

The power of the pale horse, locusts, scorpions, and serpents (5)

Revelations 6:8

KJV

⁸And I looked G1492, and behold G2400 a pale G5515 horse G2462: and his name G3686 that sat G2521 on G1883 him was Death G2288, and Hell G86 followed G190 with him. And **power G1849** was given G1325 unto them over G1909 the fourth G5067 part of the earth G1093, to kill G615 with sword G4501, and with hunger G3042, and with death G2288, and with the beasts G2342 of the earth G1093.

NKJV

⁸So I looked, and behold, a pale horse. And the name of him who sat on it was Death, and Hades followed with him. And power was given to them over a fourth of the earth, to kill with sword, with hunger, with death, and by the beasts of the earth.

NLT

⁸I looked up and saw a horse whose color was pale green. Its rider was named Death, and his companion was the Grave. These two were given authority over one-fourth of the earth, to kill with the sword and famine and disease and wild animals.

Revelation 9:3

KJV

³And there came G1831 out of the smoke G2586 locusts G200 upon the earth G1093: and unto them was given G1325 **power G1849**, as the scorpions G4651 of the earth G1093 have G2192 **power G1849**.

NKJV

³Then out of the smoke locusts came upon the earth. And to them was given power, as the scorpions of the earth have power.

NLT

³Then locusts came from the smoke and descended on the earth, and they were given power to sting like scorpions.

Revelations 9:10

KJV

¹⁰And they had G2192 tails G3769 like G3664 unto scorpions G4651, and there were stings G2759 in their tails G3769: and their **power G1849** was to hurt G91 men G444 five G4002 months G3376

NKJV

¹⁰They had tails like scorpions, and there were stings in their tails. Their power *was* to hurt men five months.

NLT

¹⁰They had tails that stung like scorpions, and for five months they had the power to torment people.

Revelations 9:19

KJV

¹⁹For their **power G1849** is in their mouth G4750, and in their tails G3769: for their tails G3769 were like G3664 unto serpents G3789, and had G2192 heads G2776, and with them they do hurt G91.

NKJV

¹⁹For their power is in their mouth and in their tails; for their tails *are* like serpents, having heads; and with them they do harm.

NLT

¹⁹Their power was in their mouths and in their tails. For their tails had heads like snakes, with the power to injure people.

CHAPTER 5

AUTHORITY
Six remaining Words sometimes translated to Authority

Katexousiazo

G2715
katexousiazo
kat-ex-oo-see-ad'-zo
From G2596 and G1850; to *have* (*wield*) *full privilege over:*—exercise authority.

G2715
katexousiazo
Thayer Definition:
1) to exercise authority, wield power
Part of Speech: verb
A Related Word by Thayer's/Strong's Number: from **G2596** and **G1850**
Total KJV Occurrences: 4
authority, 2
Matt. 20:24–25 (2); Mark 10:42
exercise, 2
Matt. 20:25; Mark 10:42

Matthew 20:25
KJV
²⁵But Jesus G2424 called G4341 them unto him, and said G2036, Ye know G1492 that the princes G758 of the Gentiles G1484 exercise G2634 dominion G2634 over them, and they that are great G3171 **exercise G2715 authority G2715** upon them.
KJV
²⁵But Jesus called them to *Himself* and said, "You know that the rulers of the Gentiles lord it over them, and those who are great exercise authority over them.
NLT
²⁵Jesus called them together and said, "You know that the rulers in this world lord it over their people, and officials flaunt their authority over those under them.

Mark 10:42
KJV
⁴²But Jesus G2424 called G4341 them to him, and saith G3004 unto them, Ye know G1492 that they which are accounted G1380 to rule G757 over the Gentiles G1484 exercise G2634 lordship G2634 over them; and their great G3173 ones **exercise G2715 authority G2715** upon them.

NKJV

⁴²But Jesus called them to *Himself* and said to them, "You know that those who are considered rulers over the Gentiles lord it over them, and their great ones exercise authority over them.

NLT

⁴²So Jesus called them together and said, "You know that the rulers in this world lord it over their people, and officials flaunt their authority over those under them.

Exousiazo

G1850

exousiazo

ex-oo-see-ad'-zo

From G1849; to *control:*—exercise authority upon, bring under the (have) power of.

G1850

exousiazo

Thayer Definition:

1) to have power or authority, use power

1a) to be master of any one, exercise authority over one

1b) to be master of the body

1b1) to have full and entire authority over the body

1b2) to hold the body subject to one's will

1c) to be brought under the power of anyone

Part of Speech: verb

A Related Word by Thayer's/Strong's Number: from **G1849**

Total KJV Occurrences: 6

power, 3

1 Cor. 6:12; 1 Cor. 7:4 (2)

authority, 1

Luke 22:25

brought, 1

1 Cor. 6:12

exercise, 1
Luke 22:25

Luke 22:25
KJV
²⁵And he said G2036 unto them, The kings G935 of the Gentiles G1484 exercise G2961 lordship G2961 over them; and they that **exercise G1850 authority G1850** upon them are called G2564 benefactors G2110.
NKJV
²⁵And He said to them, "The kings of the Gentiles exercise lordship over them, and those who exercise authority over them are called 'benefactors.'
NLT
²⁵Jesus told them, "In this world the kings and great men lord it over their people, yet they are called 'friends of the people.'

1 Corinthians 6:12
KJV
¹²All G3956 things are lawful G1832 unto me, but all G3956 things are not expedient G4851: all G3956 things are lawful G1832 for me, but I will not be **brought G1850** under G5259 **the power G1850** of any G5100.
NKJV
¹²All things are lawful for me, but all things are not helpful. All things are lawful for me, but I will not be brought under the power of any.
NLT
¹²All things are lawful for me, but all things are not helpful. All things are lawful for me, but I will not be brought under the power of any.

1 Corinthians 7:4
KJV
⁴The wife G1135 hath not **power G1850** of her own G2398 body G4983, but the husband G435: and likewise G3668 also G2532 the husband G435 hath not **power G1850** of his own G2398 body G4983, but the wife G1135.
NKJV
⁴The wife does not have authority over her own body, but the husband *does.* And likewise the husband does not have authority over his own body, but the wife *does.*

NLT

⁴The wife gives authority over her body to her husband, and the husband gives authority over his body to his wife.

Dunastes

G1413

dunastes

doo-nas'-tace

From G1410; a *ruler* or *officer:*—of great authority, mighty, potentate.

G1413

dunastes

Thayer Definition:

1) a prince, a potentate

2) a courtier, high officer, royal minister of great authority

Part of Speech: noun masculine

A Related Word by Thayer's/Strong's Number: from **G1410**

Total KJV Occurrences: 3

authority, 1

Acts 8:27

mighty, 1

Luke 1:52

potentate, 1

1 Tim. 6:15

Luke 1:52

KJV

⁵²He hath put G2507 down G2507 **the mighty G1413** from their seats G2362, and exalted G5312 them of low G5011 degree G5011.

NKJV

⁵²He has put down the mighty from *their* thrones,

And exalted *the* lowly.

NLT

⁵²He has brought down princes from their thrones and exalted the humble.

Acts 8:27
KJV
²⁷And he arose G450 and went G4198: and, behold G2400, a man G435 of Ethiopia G128, an eunuch G2135 **of great authority G1413** under Candace G2582 queen G938 of the Ethiopians G128, who G3739 had the charge G1909 of all G3956 her treasure G1047, and had come G2064 to Jerusalem G2419 for to worship G4352,
NKJV
²⁷So he arose and went. And behold, a man of Ethiopia, a eunuch of great authority under Candace the queen of the Ethiopians, who had charge of all her treasury, and had come to Jerusalem to worship,
NLT
²⁷So he started out, and he met the treasurer of Ethiopia, a eunuch of great authority under the Kandake, the queen of Ethiopia. The eunuch had gone to Jerusalem to worship,

1 Timothy 6:15
KJV
¹⁵Which G3739 in his times G5550 he shall show G1166, who G3588 is the blessed G3107 and only G3441 **Potentate G1413,** the King G935 of kings G936, and Lord G2962 of lords G2961;
NKJV
¹⁵which He will manifest in His own time, *He who is* the blessed and only Potentate, the King of kings and Lord of lords,
NLT
¹⁵For at just the right time Christ will be revealed from heaven by the blessed and only almighty God, the King of all kings and Lord of all lords.

Huperoche

G5247
huperoche
hoop-er-okh-ay'
From G5242; *prominence*, that is, (figuratively) *superiority* (in rank or character):—authority, excellency

G5247

huperoche

Thayer Definition:

1) elevation, pre-eminence, superiority

2) metaphorically excellence

Part of Speech: noun feminine

A Related Word by Thayer's/Strong's Number: from **G5242**

Total KJV Occurrences: 2

authority, 1

1 Tim. 2:2

excellency, 1

1 Cor. 2:1

1 Corinthians 2:1

KJV

¹And I, brethren G80, when I came G2064 to you, came G2064 not with **excellency G5247** of speech G3056 or G2228 of wisdom G4678, declaring G2605 unto you the testimony G3142 of God G2316.

NKJV

¹And I, brethren, when I came to you, did not come with excellence of speech or of wisdom declaring to you the testimony of God.

NLT

¹When I first came to you, dear brothers and sisters, I didn't use lofty words and impressive wisdom to tell you God's secret plan.

1 Timothy 2:2

KJV

²For kings G935, and for all G3956 that are in **authority G5247**; that we may lead G1236 a quiet G2263 and peaceable G2272 life G979 in all G3956 godliness G2150 and honesty G4587.

NKJV

²for kings and all who are in authority, that we may lead a quiet and peaceable life in all godliness and reverence.

NLT

²Pray this way for kings and all who are in authority so that we can live peaceful and quiet lives marked by godliness and dignity.

Authenteo

G831

authenteo

ow-then-teh'-o

From a compound of G846 and ἑντης hentes (obsolete; a *worker*); to *act of oneself*, that is, (figuratively) *dominate:*—usurp authority over.

G831

authenteo

Thayer Definition:

1) one who with his own hands kills another or himself

2) one who acts on his own authority, autocratic

3) an absolute master

4) to govern, exercise dominion over one

Part of Speech: verb

A Related Word by Thayer's/Strong's Number: from a compound of G846 and an obsolete hentes (a worker)

Total KJV Occurrences: 2

authority, 1

1 Tim. 2:12

usurp, 1

1 Tim. 2:12

1 Timothy 2:12

KJV

¹²But I suffer G2010 not a woman G1135 to teach G1321, nor G3761 to **usurp G831 authority G831** over the man G435, but to be in silence G2271.

NKJV

¹²And I do not permit a woman to teach or to have authority over a man, but to be in silence.

NLT

¹²I do not let women teach men or have authority over them. Let them listen quietly.

Epitage

G2003

epitage

ep-ee-tag-ay'

From G2004; an *injunction* or *decree*; by implication *authoritativeness:*— authority, commandment.

G2003

epitage

Thayer Definition:

1) an injunction, mandate, command

Part of Speech: noun feminine

A Related Word by Thayer's/Strong's Number: from **G2004**

Total KJV Occurrences: 7

commandment, 6

Rom. 16:26; 1 Cor. 7:6; 1 Cor. 7:25; 2 Cor. 8:8; 1 Tim. 1:1; Titus 1:3

authority, 1

Titus 2:15

Romans 16:26

KJV

[26]But now G3568 is made G5319 manifest G5319, and by the scriptures G1124 of the prophets G4397, according G2596 to the **commandment G2003** of the everlasting G166 God G2316, made G1107 known G1107 to all G3956 nations G1484 for the obedience G5218 of faith G4102:

NKJV

[26]but now made manifest, and by the prophetic Scriptures made known to all nations, according to the commandment of the everlasting God, for obedience to the faith—

NLT

[26]But now as the prophets foretold and as the eternal God has commanded, this message is made known to all Gentiles everywhere, so that they too might believe and obey him.

1 Corinthians 7:6

KJV

⁶But I speak G3004 this G5124 by permission G4774, and not of **commandment G2003.**

NKJV

⁶But I say this as a concession, not as a commandment.

NLT

⁶I say this as a concession, not as a command.

1 Corinthians 7:25

²⁵Now G1161 concerning G4012 virgins G3933 I have G2192 no G3756 **commandment G2003** of the Lord G2962: yet G1161 I give G1325 my judgment G1106, as one that hath obtained G1653 mercy G1653 of the Lord G2962 to be faithful G4103.

NKJV

²⁵Now concerning virgins: I have no commandment from the Lord; yet I give judgment as one whom the Lord in His mercy *has made* trustworthy.

NLT

²⁵Now regarding your question about the young women who are not yet married. I do not have a command from the Lord for them. But the Lord in his mercy has given me wisdom that can be trusted, and I will share it with you.

2 Corinthians 8:8

KJV

⁸I speak G3004 not by **commandment G2003,** but by occasion G1223 of the forwardness G4710 of others G2087, and to prove G1381 the sincerity G1103 of your G5212 love G26.

NKJV

⁸I speak not by commandment, but I am testing the sincerity of your love by the diligence of others.

NLT

⁸I am not commanding you to do this. But I am testing how genuine your love is by comparing it with the eagerness of the other churches.

1 Timothy 1:1

KJV

¹Paul G3972, an apostle G652 of Jesus G2424 Christ G5547 by the **commandment G2003** of God G2316 our Saviour G4990, and Lord G2962 Jesus G2424 Christ G5547, which G3588 is our hope G1680;

NKJV

¹Paul, an apostle of Jesus Christ, by the commandment of God our Savior and the Lord Jesus Christ, our hope,

NLT

¹This letter is from Paul, an apostle of Christ Jesus, appointed by the command of God our Savior and Christ Jesus, who gives us hope.

Titus 1:3

KJV

³But hath in due G2398 times G5550 manifested G5319 his word G3056 through G1722 preaching G2782, which G3739 is committed G4100 unto me according G2596 to the **commandment G2003** of God G2316 our Saviour G4990;

NKJV

³but has in due time manifested His word through preaching, which was committed to me according to the commandment of God our Savior;

NLT

³And now at just the right time he has revealed this message, which we announce to everyone. It is by the command of God our Savior that I have been entrusted with this work for him.

Titus 2:15

KJV

¹⁵These G5023 things speak G2980, and exhort G3870, and rebuke G1651 with all G3956 **authority G2003**. Let no G3367 man G3367 despise G4065 thee.

NKJV

¹⁵Speak these things, exhort, and rebuke with all authority. Let no one despise you.

NLT

[15]You must teach these things and encourage the believers to do them. You have the authority to correct them when necessary, so don't let anyone disregard what you say.

CHAPTER 6

AUTHORITY Five Additional Words in the New King James

Emautou, Emauto, Emauton

G1683

emautou emauto emauton

em-ow-too' em-ow-to' em-ow-ton

Genitive, dative and accusative of a compound of G1700 and G846; *of myself:*—me, mine own (self), myself.

G1683

emautou / emauto / emauton

Thayer Definition:

1) I, me, myself, etc.

Part of Speech: pronoun
A Related Word by Thayer's/Strong's Number: genitive case compound of **G1700** and **G846**
Total KJV Occurrences: 37
myself, 30
Luke 7:7; John 5:31; John 7:17; John 7:28; John 8:14; John 8:18; John 8:28; John 8:42; John 8:54; John 10:18; John 12:49; John 14:3; John 14:10; John 14:21; John 17:19; Acts 20:24; Acts 24:10; Acts 26:2; Acts 26:9; Rom. 11:4; 1 Cor. 4:4; 1 Cor. 7:6–7 (2); 1 Cor. 9:19; 2 Cor. 2:1; 2 Cor. 11:7; 2 Cor. 11:9 (2); 2 Cor. 12:5; Gal. 2:18
mine, 3
John 5:30; 1 Cor. 4:3; 1 Cor. 10:33
own, 2
1 Cor. 4:3; 1 Cor. 10:33
self, 2
John 5:30; 1 Cor. 4:3

John 17:17
KJV
17If G1437 any G5100 man will G2309 do G4160 his will G2307, he shall know G1097 of the doctrine G1322, whether G4220 it be of God G2316, or G2228 whether I speak G2980 **of myself G1683.**
NKJV
17If anyone wills to do His will, he shall know concerning the doctrine, whether it is from God or *whether* I speak on **My own _authority_**.
NLT
17Anyone who wants to do the will of God will know whether my teaching is from God or is merely my own.

John 12:49
KJV
49For I have G2192 not spoken G2980 **of myself G1683**; but the Father G3962 which G3588 sent G3992 me, he gave G1325 me a commandment G1785, what G5101 I should say G2036, and what G5101 I should speak G2980.

NKJV

⁴⁹For I have not spoken on **My own _authority_**; but the Father who sent Me gave Me a command, what I should say and what I should speak.

NLT

⁴⁹I don't speak on my own authority. The Father who sent me has commanded me what to say and how to say it.

John 14:10

KJV

¹⁰Believest G4100 thou not that I am in the Father G3962, and the Father G3962 in me? the words G4487 that I speak G2980 unto you I speak G2980 **not of myself G1683**: but the Father G3962 that dwelleth G3306 in me, he doeth G4160 the works G2041.

NKJV

¹⁰Do you not believe that I am in the Father, and the Father in Me? The words that I speak to you I do not speak on **My own _authority_;** but the Father who dwells in Me does the works.

NLT

¹⁰Don't you believe that I am in the Father and the Father is in me? The words I speak are not my own, but my Father who lives in me does his work through me.

Heautou

G1438

heautou

heh-ow-too'

(Including all the other cases); from a reflexive pronoun otherwise obsolete and the genitive (dative or accusative) of G846; him (_her, it, them,_ also [in conjunction with the personal pronoun of the other persons] _my, thy, our, your_) -self (-selves), etc.:—alone, her (own, -self), (he) himself, his (own), itself, one (to) another, our (thine) own (-selves), + that she had, their (own, own selves), (of) them (-selves), they, thyself, you, your (own, own conceits, own selves, -selves).

G1438

heautou

Thayer Definition:

1) himself, herself, itself, themselves

Part of Speech: pronoun

A Related Word by Thayer's/Strong's Number: (dative case or accusative case) of **G846**

Total KJV Occurrences: 301

himself, 114

Matt. 12:26; Matt. 12:45 (2); Matt. 13:21; Matt. 16:24; Matt. 18:4; Matt. 23:12 (2); Matt. 27:42; Mark 3:26; Mark 5:5; Mark 5:30; Mark 8:34; Mark 12:33; Mark 15:31; Luke 7:39; Luke 9:23; Luke 9:25; Luke 10:29; Luke 11:18; Luke 11:26; Luke 12:17; Luke 12:21; Luke 14:11 (2); Luke 15:15; Luke 15:17; Luke 18:3–4 (2); Luke 18:11; Luke 18:14 (2); Luke 19:12; Luke 23:2; Luke 23:35; Luke 24:12; Luke 24:27; John 2:24; John 5:18–19 (2); John 5:26 (2); John 6:61; John 7:18; John 8:22; John 11:38; John 11:51; John 13:4; John 13:32; John 16:13; John 19:7; John 21:1; John 21:7; Acts 1:3; Acts 5:36; Acts 8:9; Acts 8:34; Acts 10:17; Acts 12:11; Acts 14:17; Acts 16:27; Acts 19:31; Acts 25:4; Acts 28:16; Rom. 14:7 (2); Rom. 14:12; Rom. 14:22; Rom. 15:3; 1 Cor. 3:18; 1 Cor. 11:28–29 (2); 1 Cor. 14:4; 1 Cor. 14:28; 2 Cor. 5:18–19 (2); 2 Cor. 10:7 (2); 2 Cor. 10:18; Gal. 1:4; Gal. 2:12; Gal. 2:20; Gal.6:3–4 (2); Eph. 2:15; Eph. 5:2; Eph. 5:25; Eph. 5:27–28 (2); Eph. 5:33; Phil. 2:7–8 (2); Phil. 3:21; 2 Thess. 2:4 (2); 1 Tim. 2:6; 2 Tim. 2:13; 2 Tim. 2:21; Titus 2:14 (2); Heb. 5:3–5 (4); Heb. 6:13; Heb. 7:27; Heb. 9:7; Heb. 9:14; Heb. 9:25; James 1:24; James 1:27; 1 John 3:3; 1 John 5:18

themselves, 57

Matt. 9:3; Matt. 14:15; Matt. 16:7; Matt. 19:12; Matt. 21:25; Matt. 21:38; Mark 2:8; Mark 4:17; Mark 6:36; Mark 6:51; Mark 9:8; Mark 9:10; Mark 10:26; Mark 11:31; Mark 12:7; Mark 14:4; Mark 16:3; Luke 7:30; Luke 7:49; Luke 18:9; Luke 20:5; Luke 20:14; Luke 20:20; Luke 22:23; Luke 23:12; John 7:35; John 11:55; John 12:19; Acts 23:12; Acts 23:21; Acts 28:29; Rom. 1:24; Rom. 1:27; Rom. 2:14; Rom. 13:2; 1 Cor. 16:15; 2 Cor. 5:15; 2 Cor. 10:12 (5); Eph. 4:19; Phil. 2:3; 1 Tim. 2:9; 1 Tim. 3:13; 1 Tim.

6:10; 1 Tim. 6:19; 2 Tim. 4:3; Heb. 6:6; 1 Pet. 1:12; 1 Pet. 3:5; 2 Pet. 2:1; Jude 1:12; Jude 1:19; Rev. 6:15; Rev. 8:6

yourselves, 37

Matt. 3:9; Matt. 16:8; Matt. 23:31; Matt. 25:9; Mark 9:33; Mark 9:50; Mark 13:9; Luke 3:8; Luke 12:33; Luke 12:57; Luke 16:9; Luke 16:15; Luke 17:3; Luke 17:14; Luke 21:34; Luke 22:17; Luke 23:28; Acts 5:35; Acts 13:46; Acts 15:29; Acts 20:28; Rom. 6:11; Rom. 6:13; Rom. 6:16; Rom. 12:19; 2 Cor. 7:11; 2 Cor. 13:5; Eph. 5:19; 1 Thess. 5:13; 1 Thess. 5:15; Heb. 10:34; James 2:4; 1 Pet. 4:8; 1 John 5:21; 2 John 1:8; Jude 1:20–21 (2)

own, 24

Luke 14:26; Luke 22:71; John 20:10; Acts 7:21; Rom. 4:19; Rom. 8:3; Rom. 11:25; Rom. 12:16; Rom. 16:4; Rom. 16:18; 1 Cor. 6:19; 1 Cor. 7:2; 1 Cor. 10:24; 1 Cor. 10:29; 1 Cor. 13:5; Gal. 6:4; Eph. 5:28–29 (2); Phil. 2:4; Phil. 2:12; 1 Thess. 2:8; 2 Thess. 3:12; Jude 1:13; Jude 1:18

ourselves, 21

Acts 23:14; Rom. 8:23; Rom. 15:1; 1 Cor. 11:31; 2 Cor. 1:9 (2); 2 Cor. 3:1; 2 Cor. 3:5 (2); 2 Cor. 4:2; 2 Cor. 4:5 (2); 2 Cor. 5:12; 2 Cor. 6:4; 2 Cor. 7:1; 2 Cor. 10:12 (2); 2 Cor. 10:14; 2 Thess. 3:9; Heb. 10:25; 1 John 1:8

itself, 9

Matt. 6:34; Matt. 12:25 (2); Mark 3:24–25 (2); Luke 11:17; John 15:4; Rom. 14:14; Eph. 4:16

your, 8

Luke 21:30; Rom. 11:25; 1 Cor. 6:19; 2 Cor. 13:5 (2); Eph. 5:25; Phil. 2:12; James 1:22

another, 7

Mark 9:10; 1 Cor. 6:7; Eph. 4:32; Col. 3:13; Col. 3:16; Heb. 3:13; 1 Pet. 4:10

one, 6

1 Cor. 6:7; Eph. 4:32; Col. 3:13; Col. 3:16; Heb. 3:13; 1 Pet. 4:10

herself, 5

Matt. 9:21; Luke 1:24; Rev. 2:20; Rev. 19:7 (2)

selves, 4

Luke 21:30; 2 Cor. 13:5 (3)

thyself, 3
John 18:34; Rom. 13:9; Gal. 5:14
conceits, 2
Rom. 11:25; Rom. 12:16
alone, 1
James 2:16–17 (2)
home, 1
John 20:10
thine, 1
1 Cor. 10:29
troubled, 1
John 11:33

John 11:51

KJV

[51]And this G5124 spake G2036 he **not of himself G1438**: but being G5607 high G749 priest G749 that year G1763, he prophesied G4395 that Jesus G2424 should G3195 die G599 for that nation G1484;

NKJV

[51]Now this he did not say on **his own _authority_:** but being high priest that year he prophesied that Jesus would die for the nation,

NLT

[51]He did not say this on his own; as high priest at that time he was led to prophesy that Jesus would die for the entire nation.

John 16:13

KJV

[13]Howbeit when G3752 he, the Spirit G4151 of truth G225, is come G2064, he will guide G3594 you into G1519 all G3956 truth G225: for he shall not speak G2980 of **himself G1438**; but whatsoever G3745–G302 he shall hear G191, that shall he speak G2980: and he will show G312 you things to come G2064.

NKJV

[13]However, when He, the Spirit of truth, has come, He will guide you into all truth; for He will not speak on **His own _authority_**, but whatever He hears He will speak; and He will tell you things to come.

NLT

[13]When the Spirit of truth comes, he will guide you into all truth. He will not speak on his own but will tell you what he has heard. He will tell you about the future.

Archon

G758

archon

ar'-khone

Present participle of G757; a _first_ (in rank or power):—chief (ruler), magistrate, prince, ruler.

G758

archon

Thayer Definition:

1) a ruler, commander, chief, leader

Part of Speech: noun masculine

A Related Word by Thayer's/Strong's Number: present participle of **G757**

Total KJV Occurrences: 38

rulers, 14

Luke 23:13; Luke 23:35; Luke 24:20; John 7:26; John 7:48; John 12:42; Acts 3:17; Acts 4:5; Acts 4:8; Acts 13:26–27 (2); Acts 14:5; Acts 16:19; Rom. 13:3

prince, 8

Matt. 9:34; Matt. 12:24; Mark 3:22; John 12:31; John 14:30; John 16:11; Eph. 2:2; Rev. 1:5

ruler, 8

Matt. 9:18; Luke 8:41; Luke 18:18; John 3:1; Acts 7:27; Acts 7:35 (2); Acts 23:5

chief, 3
Luke 11:15; Luke 14:1; John 12:42
princes, 3
Matt. 20:25; 1 Cor. 2:6; 1 Cor. 2:8
magistrate, 1
Luke 12:58
ruler's, 1
Matt. 9:23

Acts 16:19
KJV
[19]And when her masters G2962 saw G1492 that the hope G1680 of their gains G2039 was gone G1831, they caught G1949 Paul G3972 and Silas G4609, and drew G1670 them into G1519 the marketplace G58 **unto the rulers G758,**
NKJV
[19]But when her masters saw that their hope of profit was gone, they seized Paul and Silas and dragged *them* into the marketplace **to the authorities.**
NLT
[19]Her masters' hopes of wealth were now shattered, so they grabbed Paul and Silas and dragged them before the authorities at the marketplace.

Dunatos

G1415
dunatos
doo-nat-os'
From G1410; *powerful* or *capable* (literally or figuratively); neuter *possible:*—able, could, (that is) mighty (man), possible, power, strong.

G1415
dunatos
Thayer Definition:
1) able, powerful, mighty, strong
1a) mighty in wealth and influence
1b) strong in soul

1b1) to bear calamities and trials with fortitude and patience
1b2) strong in Christian virtue
2) to be able (to do something)
2a) mighty, excelling in something
2b) having power for something
Part of Speech: adjective
A Related Word by Thayer's/Strong's Number: from **G1410**
Total KJV Occurrences: 35
possible, 13
Matt. 19:26; Matt. 24:24; Matt. 26:39; Mark 9:23; Mark 10:27; Mark 13:22; Mark 14:35–36 (2); Luke 18:27; Acts 2:24; Acts 20:16; Rom. 12:18; Gal. 4:15
able, 10
Luke 14:31; Acts 25:5; Rom. 4:21; Rom. 11:23; Rom. 14:4; 2 Cor. 9:8; 2 Tim. 1:12; Titus 1:9; Heb. 11:19; James 3:2
mighty, 7
Luke 1:49; Luke 24:19; Acts 7:22; Acts 18:24; 1 Cor. 1:26; 2 Cor. 10:4; Rev. 6:15
strong, 3
Rom. 15:1; 2 Cor. 12:10; 2 Cor. 13:9
could, 1
Acts 11:17
power, 1
Rom. 9:22

Acts 25:5
KJV
⁵Let them therefore G3767, said G5346 he, which among G1722 **you are able G1415,** go G4782 down G4782 with me, and accuse G2723 this G846 man G435, if G1487 there be any G1536 wickedness G824 in him.
NKJV
⁵"Therefore," he said, "let those **who have authority** among you go down with *me* and accuse this man, to see if there is any fault in him."
NLT
⁵So he said, "Those of you in authority can return with me. If Paul has done anything wrong, you can make your accusations."

Kuriotes

G2963
kuriotes
koo-ree-ot'-ace
From G2962; *mastery*, that is, (concretely and collectively) *rulers:*—dominion, government.

G2963
kuriotes
Thayer Definition:
1) dominion, power, lordship
2) in the NT: one who possesses dominion
Part of Speech: noun feminine
A Related Word by Thayer's/Strong's Number: from **G2962**
Total KJV Occurrences: 4
dominion, 2
Eph. 1:21; Jude 1:8
dominions, 1
Col. 1:16
government, 1
2 Pet. 2:10

Jude 1:8
KJV
⁸Likewise G3668 also G2532 these G3778 filthy dreamers G1797 defile G3392 the flesh G4561, despise G114 **dominion G2963**, and speak G987 evil G987 of dignities G1391.
NKJV
⁸Likewise also these dreamers defile the flesh, reject **authority,** and speak evil of dignitaries.
NLT
⁸In the same way, these people—who claim authority from their dreams—live immoral lives, defy authority, and scoff at supernatural beings.

CHAPTER 7

Dunamis

Greek definitions from
Strong's and Thayer's dictionaries

G1411

δύναμις

dunamis

doo'-nam-is

From G1410; *force* (literally or figuratively); specifically miraculous *power* (usually by implication a *miracle* itself):—ability, abundance, meaning, might (-ily, -y, -y deed), (worker of) miracle (-s), power, strength, violence, mighty (wonderful) work.

G1411

δύναμις

dunamis

Thayer Definition:

1) strength power, ability

1a) inherent power, power residing in a thing by virtue of its nature, or which a person or thing exerts and puts forth

1b) power for performing miracles

1c) moral power and excellence of soul

1d) the power and influence which belong to riches and wealth

1e) power and resources arising from numbers
1f) power consisting in or resting upon armies, forces, hosts
Part of Speech: noun feminine
A Related Word by Thayer's/Strong's Number: from **G1410**
Total KJV Occurrences: 123
power, 71
Matt. 6:13; Matt. 24:29–30 (2); Matt. 26:64; Mark 9:1; Mark 12:24; Mark 13:26; Mark 14:62; Luke 1:17; Luke 1:35; Luke 4:14; Luke 4:36; Luke 5:17; Luke 9:1; Luke 10:19; Luke 21:27; Luke 22:69; Luke 24:49; Acts 1:8; Acts 3:12; Acts 4:7; Acts 4:33; Acts 6:8; Acts 8:10; Acts 10:38; Rom. 1:4; Rom. 1:16; Rom. 1:20; Rom. 9:17; Rom. 15:13; Rom. 15:19; 1 Cor. 1:18; 1 Cor. 1:24; 1 Cor. 2:4–5 (2); 1 Cor. 4:19–20 (2); 1 Cor. 5:4; 1 Cor. 6:14; 1 Cor. 15:24; 1 Cor. 15:43; 2 Cor. 6:7 (2); 2 Cor. 8:3 (2); 2 Cor. 12:9; 2 Cor. 13:4 (2); Eph. 1:19; Eph. 3:7; Eph. 3:20; Phil. 3:10; 1 Thess. 1:5; 2 Thess. 1:11; 2 Thess. 2:9; 2 Tim. 1:7–8 (2); 2 Tim. 3:5; Heb. 1:3; Heb. 7:16; 1 Pet. 1:5; 2 Pet. 1:3; 2 Pet. 1:16; Rev. 7:11–12 (3); Rev. 11:17; Rev. 13:2; Rev. 15:8; Rev. 17:13; Rev. 19:1
mighty, 14
Matt. 11:20–21 (2); Matt. 11:23; Matt. 13:54; Matt. 13:58; Mark 6:2 (2); Mark 6:5; Mark 6:14; Luke 10:13; Luke 19:37; Rom. 15:19; 2 Cor. 12:12; 2 Thess. 1:7
miracles, 8
Acts 2:22; Acts 8:13; Acts 19:11; 1 Cor. 12:10; 1 Cor. 12:28–29 (2); Gal. 3:5; Heb. 2:4
strength, 7
1 Cor. 15:56; 2 Cor. 12:8–9 (2); Heb. 11:11; Rev. 1:16; Rev. 3:8; Rev. 12:10
powers, 6
Matt. 24:29; Luke 21:25–26 (2); Rom. 8:38; Heb. 6:5; 1 Pet. 3:22
might, 4
Eph. 1:21; Eph. 3:16; Col. 1:11; 2 Pet. 2:11
virtue, 3
Mark 5:30; Luke 6:19; Luke 8:46
ability, 1
Matt. 25:15

abundance, 1
Rev. 18:3
deeds, 1
2 Cor. 12:12
meaning, 1
1 Cor. 14:11
mightily, 1
Col. 1:29
miracle, 1
Mark 9:39
violence, 1
Heb. 11:34
wonderful, 1
Matt. 7:22
work, 1
Mark 6:5
workers, 1
1 Cor. 12:29

CPSIA information can be obtained
at www.ICGtesting.com
Printed in the USA
BVOW08s0813010517
482720BV00001B/2/P

9 781478 779193